TEST YOUR EQ

Find Out How *Emotionally Intelligent* You Really Are

MARK DAVIS, PH.D.

 New American Library

New American Library
Published by New American Library, a division of
Penguin Group (USA) Inc., 375 Hudson Street,
New York, New York 10014, USA
Penguin Group (Canada), 90 Eglinton Avenue East, Suite 700, Toronto,
Ontario M4P 2Y3, Canada (a division of Pearson Penguin Canada Inc.)
Penguin Books Ltd., 80 Strand, London WC2R 0RL, England
Penguin Ireland, 25 St. Stephen's Green, Dublin 2,
Ireland (a division of Penguin Books Ltd.)
Penguin Group (Australia), 250 Camberwell Road, Camberwell, Victoria 3124,
Australia (a division of Pearson Australia Group Pty. Ltd.)
Penguin Books India Pvt. Ltd., 11 Community Centre, Panchsheel Park,
New Delhi-110 017, India
Penguin Group (NZ), cnr Airborne and Rosedale Roads, Albany,
Auckland 1310, New Zealand (a division of Pearson New Zealand Ltd.)
Penguin Books (South Africa) (Pty.) Ltd., 24 Sturdee Avenue,
Rosebank, Johannesburg 2196, South Africa

Penguin Books Ltd., Registered Offices:
80 Strand, London WC2R 0RL, England

Published by New American Library, a division of Penguin Group (USA) Inc.
Published by arrangement with Piatkus Books Ltd. For information address
Piatkus Books Ltd., 5 Windmill Street, London, England W1T 2JA.

First New American Library Printing, August 2005
10 9 8 7 6 5 4 3 2 1

Copyright © Mark Davis, 2004
All rights reserved

NEW AMERICAN LIBRARY and logo are trademarks of
Penguin Group (USA) Inc.

LIBRARY OF CONGRESS CATALOGING-IN-PUBLICATION DATA

Davis, Mark H.
    Test your EQ: find out how emotionally intelligent you really are/Mark Davis.
        p. cm.
    Includes bibliographical references and index.
    ISBN 0-451-21530-3
    1. Emotional intelligence. 2. Self-report inventories. I. Title.
    BF576.D38 2005
    152.4—dc22   2005047865

Printed in the United States of America

PUBLISHER'S NOTE
While the author has made every effort to provide accurate telephone
numbers and Internet addresses at the time of publication, neither the
publisher nor the author assumes any responsibility for errors, or for changes
that occur after publication. Further, publisher does not have any control
over and does not assume any responsibility for author or third-party Web
sites or their content.

CONTENTS

1

EMOTIONAL INTELLIGENCE:
what it is and how to measure it

A YOUNG GIRL sits staring at the marshmallow in front of her. She has been told that she can either eat this marshmallow right now, or have *two* marshmallows if she is willing to wait five minutes. Having two marshmallows is better than having one, so the choice seems easy. However, five minutes turns out to be a long time, especially when the tasty snack is right in front of you. The girl stares at it, her eyes wide. She turns around in her chair for a few seconds so that she cannot see the marshmallow, but before long turns back around. She picks it up, turns it over, and then brings it to her face and inhales deeply. She puts it back down, and puts her hands over her eyes. Then, with a sigh, she reaches for the marshmallow and opens her mouth....

Nigel, a middle-level executive, is perplexed. Smart, well educated and hardworking, he is nevertheless currently struggling with the biggest assignment of his career. Chosen to lead a task force consisting of the heads of several different departments, Nigel is terribly frustrated. Each of the task force members has a personal agenda, and all seem suspicious of one another. Despite his best efforts, Nigel is unable to persuade the group to work together. Unless something changes, this assignment is going to be an utter failure—more to the point, it will be *his* failure, and a substantial black mark on his currently spotless résumé....

Nick is at a loss. His marriage is crumbling and there seems to be nothing he can do about it. His wife is bitterly unhappy with him, but he has only the vaguest understanding why. He is sober, dependable and faithful—even Susie acknowledges that—but he is also emotionally distant and uncommunicative. Susie's moods are an almost complete mystery to him, and he still can't quite understand how she can get so upset about the fact that he doesn't say much. It just doesn't seem fair. What's the big deal about emotions, anyway?

Good question.

This book is about *emotional intelligence*—defined as the ability to recognize, understand, regulate and effectively use emotions in our lives. Each of the three people described above is in some way wrestling with problems for which emotional intelligence would be helpful. The little girl with the marshmallow (an actual experiment, by the way) is trying to resist the temptation of an immediate reward; Nigel is attempting to manage the emotional climate in his task force; and Nick is struggling to find a way to satisfy the emotional needs of his wife. In each instance, the problem facing the person is one of *feelings*—how to control, use or express them in a way that produces good outcomes. To really understand the concept of emotional intelligence, however, it is necessary to take a step or two back and see where this idea came from.

What is intelligence?

The concept of intelligence has a very long history; in fact, it is probably as old as humanity itself. Even the oldest recorded human stories, such as the Sumerian *Epic of Gilgamesh* (more than five thousand years old), describe some characters as "wise," and others as, well, decidedly less so. Biblical stories depict striking examples of intelligence (that of King Solomon, for example) and foolishness (that of Noah's neighbors, and the Pharaoh). It seems that we humans have long embraced the idea that some people are better at decision making than others. These people may possess the same information as the rest of us, but when they are through weighing, evaluating and processing it, the conclusions they reach are just *better* than the conclusions reached by others.

Despite the widespread recognition that intelligence as a personal characteristic exists, it was not until the end of the nineteenth century that serious efforts were made to formally measure this quality. These efforts were spurred initially by the work of Francis Galton, but it was Alfred Binet who in 1905 developed the prototype of the modern intelligence test. Binet's test was developed in order to help the French educational system identify children with subnormal mental abilities so that they might receive special instruction. Over time, however, and especially as the test was translated into English and used in the United States, the focus shifted to quantifying the intelligence of *all* children. The development of a tool for measuring intelligence turned out to be wildly popular, and such testing became widespread, especially in America. (Because the intelligence score in the Binet method was calculated as a ratio of "mental age" over "chronological age," the resulting score was known as the "intelligence quotient," or IQ.)

While use of intelligence testing since that time has sometimes been controversial, one fundamental assumption of the IQ approach has never really been questioned: the idea that intelligence is a measure of how people handle abstract information. That is, intelligence was always considered to be about the way in which people evaluate ideas, use logic, manipulate numbers, recognize similarities, draw inferences and grasp new concepts. All of these tasks are clearly in the realm of the cognitive and the intellectual, and when IQ tests evaluate people on these skills, they produce scores that are based completely on *cognitive* abilities. For the most part these tests completely ignore the large part of human experience represented by feelings, desires and motives. Intelligence measures have therefore always focused on one particular aspect of the human experience—an important one, to be sure, but by no means the only one.

There was, however, one fly in the ointment. Despite the widespread popularity of intelligence testing, and the exponential growth of the intelligence testing movement, it turned out that in some situations intelligence was not as powerful a determinant of behavior as we might think. To be sure, IQ is one of the strongest predictors of performance at school, and this is certainly important. However, when it comes to success in other areas of life, IQ's influence is not always as large. For example, research that has examined the link between IQ and job performance has produced somewhat mixed findings.

Some research suggests that IQ accounts for as much as 25 percent of the variability in job performance, but in other studies the estimates are much lower—as low as 5 or 10 percent. Even if the 25 percent figure is accepted, however, this would mean that three-quarters of the variability that we see in job performance is *not* the result of IQ, but comes from somewhere else. If IQ, as important as it is, does not determine this kind of success, then what does?

One answer, you will not be surprised to learn, may lie in the way that people use and understand emotions.

The role of the emotions in intelligence

Although the IQ movement essentially excluded any consideration of emotion, it was not as though *all* psychologists had been ignoring emotions. Indeed, for more than a century researchers and theorists have been attempting to understand emotions: what causes them, what their purpose is and what their consequences are. However, for many years the dominant view of emotions was that they were almost completely separate from intelligence, or were even actively antagonistic to intelligence. One common image of emotions during this time was that they generally tended to distract people from a calm and rational (that is, "intelligent") focus on abstract information.

It was really not until the 1980s that a different conception of emotions began to develop: the idea that emotions do not necessarily interfere with intelligent thinking and behavior, but might in fact be able to contribute to human intelligence. In fact, one important idea that developed during this time was the notion that emotions are a *kind of information*. What this means is that people use their emotions—just as they use more familiar kinds of information—in order to make judgments about the world. What kind of information do emotions provide? Emotions, according to this view, provide us with information about *value*. They are a kind of shorthand signal to ourselves that we have evaluated something in the environment in an either positive or negative fashion.

As an example, if you settle in behind the wheel of your car one morning and suddenly notice a huge swarm of angry bees in the backseat, this will rather reliably produce the emotion of fear. That feeling of fear is a strong and simple piece of information based on your evaluation that "being this close to angry bees will lead to great pain, and is a *BAD IDEA*." The value of having such a simple and dramatic emotional summary of your evaluation is that it prompts swift and effective action ("Get out of the car!"). The key point, however, is that the emotion you are feeling is not random, but is the logical result of correctly perceiving a threat in the environment. The emotion you are feeling is therefore a useful piece of information about your world, and rather than interfering with your ability to react intelligently, it aids you in this endeavor.

Of course, most of our emotions are not quite as simple or dramatic as this. Most of our feelings are more subtle, and many are more complex, but the kind of information they provide us with can be very useful in interpreting the world. In fact, even the bees in the back seat will prompt more emotional responses than the simple fear reaction already described. Once you have safely escaped from your four-wheeled buzzing hive of death, other emotions will arise, most particularly curiosity ("Where the devil did those bees come from?"), which will help prompt a thorough investigation to prevent any further occurrences of the event.

Emotional intelligence: two views

The notion that emotions are really a kind of information helped set the stage for the appearance in 1990 of the fully fledged concept of emotional intelligence. Two American psychologists—Peter Salovey and John Mayer—were the first to use this term, and their scholarly work on this topic has provided the foundation for all later work in this area.

In their influential 1990 paper, Salovey and Mayer defined emotional intelligence (EQ) as a form of intelligence "that involves the ability to monitor one's own and others' feelings and emotions, to discriminate among them and to use this information to guide one's thoughts and actions." (Even though emotional intelligence measures do not involve the same kind of "mental/ chronological" ratio as Binet's IQ scores, the most common shorthand term for emotional intelligence, EQ, mimics the abbreviation for the original "intelligence quotient.")

Underlying Salovey and Mayer's approach was the belief that there is a small number of specific skills, all of which have to do with either accuracy or effectiveness: *accuracy* at perceiving and understanding emotional states in the self and in others, and *effectiveness* at regulating, controlling and using these emotions in order to achieve one's goals. In particular, Salovey and Mayer propose that there are four fundamental aspects to emotional intelligence:

- Recognizing emotions
- Understanding emotions
- Regulating emotions
- Using emotions

As you will see in later chapters, these skills can lead to a number of positive outcomes for the individual who possesses them. Lacking these skills, in contrast, can create some real difficulties.

The usual fate of academic psychological research, even very good research, is dismally predictable. It is first published in professional journals and eventually read by relatively small numbers of colleagues, students and the occasional unfortunate family member. What happened in the case of the emotional intelligence research was very different. What happened was Daniel Goleman.

For a number of years Goleman was the leading science writer for the *New York Times*. In that capacity, he wrote about research related to emotional intelligence several times, and in 1995 he published an entire book (*Emotional Intelligence*) on the subject. It was a tremendous success, sold millions of copies, spawned additional books on the topic by Goleman and others (like this one), and popularized the notion of emotional intelligence to a much greater degree than is usual with traditional psychological research. Goleman, however, took a somewhat broader view of emotional intelligence than did Salovey and Mayer.

Goleman's definition of emotional intelligence, which has evolved over the years, proposes four broad domains of EQ (self-awareness, social awareness, self-management and relationship management), with twenty specific "competencies" falling into one of these four domains. For example, the domain of self-management is said to contain the six competencies of self-control, trustworthiness, conscientiousness, adaptability, achievement drive and initiative.

Goleman's conception of EQ specifies twenty different competencies, and he thus takes a substantially broader view of EQ than do Salovey and Mayer. In particular, some of the competencies identified by Goleman may not really be abilities at all (and thus would not technically qualify as a kind of intelligence), but may reflect personality traits instead. At the level of the four general domains, however, the two approaches do resemble each other. In this book I for the most part follow the original Salovey and Mayer approach, organizing the chapters around the four basic skills those authors identified.

Floors and ceilings

The broad appeal of EQ—its bright promise—is that it might provide an answer to the question posed earlier: what accounts for the large part of success in the realms of work and family that is *not* due to IQ? If the ability to understand and use emotions really can be considered a form of intelligence separate from traditional IQ, this ability may indeed provide us with a way to understand how people with equal IQ levels can nevertheless differ so much in their ability to succeed in life.

The evidence that emotional intelligence can explain success beyond that accounted for by IQ is currently somewhat tentative, but it does suggest that EQ is providing a piece of the picture that IQ does not. One useful way to think about the way that IQ and EQ may combine to influence life effectiveness is this. In a way, IQ provides us with a "floor" for our accomplishments. For example, there are certain kinds of work that people simply will not be able to do without a certain degree of traditional IQ. Being a doctor or scientist, or a high-level executive, requires a certain minimal level of intelligence, and without it a person will almost never succeed in these fields. In this sense, then, IQ is a tremendously important determinant of success.

But what about those people who "made the cut"— who possess the requisite IQ and are now doctors, scientists and high-level executives? For these people, success within their profession relative to their peers is *not* due much to IQ, because all of these people have more than enough. Differences among these people will be due to other factors, such as an ability to effectively maneuver through social situations, read the emotional cues of peers, clients and bosses, and persevere in the face of emotional setbacks.

While IQ provides the floor for these people's accomplishments, therefore, EQ in a sense determines the "ceiling"—that is, it determines how high they can rise compared to others with the same cognitive and technical skills. The exact contribution of IQ and EQ to someone's life success depends on the particular area of life being considered; some situations emphasize IQ and technical skills, while others emphasize EQ and social skills. In almost all situations, though—from being a surgeon to being a good parent—both IQ and EQ would seem to have significant roles to play in determining our success.

Can EQ be measured?

Emotional intelligence can be hard to measure—in fact, some psychologists doubt that it can be assessed at all. However, many believe that it can be measured, but that there are obstacles to be overcome in doing so. The biggest problem is that the easiest way to measure EQ— through what are called self-report measures—is probably the weakest way to do it. Self-report scales ask the person who is taking the test to report on his or her abilities, skills and behaviors. In the case of EQ, for example, such scales would ask how effective the person is in recognizing emotions, understanding emotions, and so on. These tests rely on the fact that people can be accurate reporters about their own skills and abilities.

There are, however, some problems with this assumption:

- People often tend to exaggerate their own accomplishments and minimize their shortcomings; as a result, self-report tests often provide an inflated picture of someone's skills or abilities.
- Even if people are brutally honest in their self-reports, they frequently lack accurate insight. That is, people may not only shade the truth in their answers, but also in many cases they may not even know the truth to start with.

For both of these reasons, self-report measures of EQ, while valuable, should not be used as the only measure of EQ.

One solution to the problems of self-report measures is to use "multirater tests." In this approach, questions about a person's behavior are answered not by them, but by people who know them. The individual's friends, coworkers or family members therefore provide their estimates of how the individual usually acts. The advantage of such multirater questionnaires is twofold. One is that other people are less prone to shade their answers than the individual would be in order to portray themselves in a favorable light. The second advantage is that other people are often in a better position to witness and accurately evaluate how skillful the individual is in social interaction.

A final approach is to use performance tests to measure EQ. Performance tests do not ask the test takers to report on their typical behavior; nor do they ask others to do so. Instead, these tests present test takers with practical problems and ask them to figure out the correct answers. Thus, instead of asking you to report on how good your EQ skills are, the tests ask you to actually *demonstrate* those skills. These tests are not as vulnerable to the problems facing self-report and multirater tests, but they are much more difficult to construct.

How is EQ currently measured?

The most widely used and respected measures of emotional intelligence currently in use are commercial instruments. That is, it costs money to take these tests and have them scored—often a very substantial amount of money. As a result, these scales are most typically used by large organizations rather than by individuals. Some of the tests are purely self-report measures, others are multirater tests and some of these measures also include a performance component.

These commercial instruments are typically the result of years of development—of testing, refinement and validation—all of which is costly. Tests that have this level of time and effort invested in them will always be relatively expensive, and as a result not easily available to ordinary individuals. How, then, can such individuals assess their own EQ levels?

Until now, such individual assessments have been difficult or even impossible, and that is the reason for this book. The heart of the book is a series of tests, developed specially for this project, which measure the different skills and abilities that make up EQ. For the first time, anyone has a chance to evaluate himself or herself on all of the key areas encompassed by the broad term emotional intelligence.

So what's the catch?

How can this book provide tests of EQ without the expense of the commercial instruments? The answer is simple; the tests in this book have not gone through the elaborate and expensive development and validation process of the commercial instruments.

Because the tests do not have the same weight of scientific evidence behind them as those used in commerce, you need to exercise caution when interpreting your scores. However, steps have been taken to make the tests as accurate a measure as possible of EQ abilities:

- In creating the tests, I have drawn upon more than two decades of experience as a research psychologist, and in particular on my participation in developing well-respected and widely used measures of dispositional empathy and conflict resolution styles.

- Two specific strategies were employed to maximize validity. Whenever possible I have included a performance component in the tests to reduce the problems of simple self-report measures. Additionally, in many cases the tests are meant to be completed not only by the test taker but also by friends and family members, so that the self-report tests are supported by multirater information.

At the end of the book, the section entitled "Scoring and Interpreting Your EQ Tests" provides the answers to the various tests, explains how to score them, and gives more detail about how to most appropriately interpret the scores.

The plan for the book

The remainder of this book is organized around the four components of EQ identified earlier: the abilities to recognize, understand, regulate and use emotions. These components all influence one another, but it is also possible to think of them arranged, pyramid-style, with the most basic and fundamental skills at the bottom, and with "higher" skills depending on the "lower" ones (see diagram opposite).

Each of the four components is accorded its own

chapter, in which it is discussed in some depth. At the end of each chapter is a series of tests designed to measure your ability in that area. Chapters 2 to 5 therefore allow you to learn about, and then test, your own EQ. Chapter 6 presents information that will be helpful if you would like to improve your EQ in any of these areas. Finally, the resources section contains lists of books, articles and Web sites that you may find useful.

Figure 1.1: Emotional Intelligence

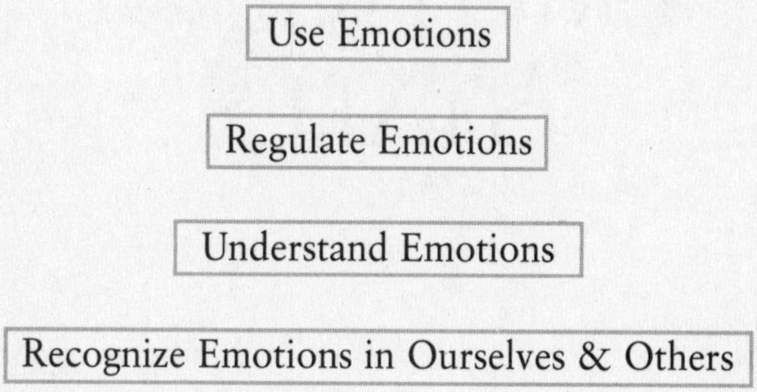

Use Emotions

Regulate Emotions

Understand Emotions

Recognize Emotions in Ourselves & Others

2

RECOGNIZING EMOTIONAL STATES

THE MOST FUNDAMENTAL skill contributing to emotional intelligence is the ability to *accurately recognize emotional states*. The reason for this is simple: an inability to recognize an emotion for what it is, or to correctly distinguish one emotion from another, essentially makes all the other skills useless. How can you successfully regulate or control emotions, for example, if you don't know what you are regulating? How can you use emotions to enhance your success if you don't know what your emotions *are*? Just as it is essential for children to learn the alphabet before they can move on to reading and writing, the ability to accurately recognize, label and describe emotions is the cornerstone for all of the other, more advanced uses of emotions.

To make this point more vividly, consider the extreme case of people who are totally unable to recognize moods and emotions. The psychological condition known as alexithymia consists of an inability to describe or recognize emotions. People with this disorder are typically unable to describe their own emotional states to others or even to themselves; they seem to completely lack an ability to represent their private feelings in a way (such as language) that is understandable to themselves or to other people.

As you might expect, such a disorder puts the individual in a very unusual situation. Alexithymics may, for example, experience bodily changes (butterflies in the stomach, racing heart) but at the same time have no idea that this means they are feeling anxiety. They may watch a sad film and feel a vague sense of unpleasantness, but not recognize that the particular emotion they are feeling is sadness. As far as they are concerned, it could be fear, anger, jealousy . . . or heartburn.

Obviously, a disorder like this is very uncommon, and you are unlikely to have difficulties this severe, but "normal" people also differ considerably in how accurately they can recognize emotional states, and this kind of everyday variation is what EQ encompasses.

Although emotional recognition is clearly important, so far we have not paid much attention to one rather critical issue, namely the *location* of the emotion we are trying to identify. According to theories about emotional intelligence, there are two primary places where such emotions might be: in other people, and in ourselves.

Recognition of emotional states within the self

It might seem odd to talk about an inability to recognize your own feelings. For those of us who are not suffering from alexithymia, nothing in the world seems more natural than having an emotion and knowing what it is. We can all recall many times when our moods were so strong (the birth of a child) or so clear (getting an unexpected raise) that we had absolutely no difficulty at all in recognizing what they were. Because it is so easy to think of such times, it is tempting to imagine that *all* your emotions are easy to identify. Tempting, perhaps, but not true. Rather than producing strong and clear emotional responses, some situations instead provoke emotions that are rather mild; other situations provoke not a single, clearly labeled response, but a complex mixture of feelings. In either case, the task of correctly identifying your true feelings can be difficult, and some people tend to be better at it than others.

Why is an ability to recognize your own emotional states useful? There are many possible reasons, and here are three key ones.

Emotions give you information about your judgments

The first reason is based on an argument raised in chapter 1 (see page 6): that emotions are a kind of information. Because emotions clearly tell you how you are evaluating something—people, things, situations, ideas — an accurate understanding of your emotions means that you have more accurate information about your evaluations. Accurately knowing your emotions gives you better insight into what you like, dislike or are ambivalent about.

Imagine, for example, someone who is interviewing two job applicants. Both of the applicants appear on paper to have the necessary skills and experience, but the interviewer is sensitive to subtle feelings that she has while interviewing them; in one case the feelings are positive and in the other negative. The interviewer may not even know what has triggered the feelings, but the feelings are information—they say something (perhaps important) about the interviewer's evaluation of each candidate. Another interviewer, who is less able to recognize her subtle emotional states, may ignore this information because she cannot distinguish between the two sets of feelings.

Thus, one reason why accurately recognizing your own feelings is important is that it provides you with information about your judgments. Once you have that information, however, what do you do with it?

Emotions give you clues on how to behave

Having information about your judgments provides you with important cues about the most appropriate ways to behave in given situations. Many emotions are signals to you about where to direct your attention and how to direct your energies; if you do not accurately identify the emotion, you will not act in the most appropriate ways. For example, the feeling of shame typically occurs as the result of violating some social expectation; we feel ashamed when we let our friends down (perhaps through disloyalty), or bring dishonor to our family (perhaps with an egregiously bad haircut).

These unpleasant feelings are a signal that some kind of violation has occurred, and the signal spurs you to direct your attention and efforts toward repairing the damage. A failure to accurately recognize and label these feelings may result in the important repair work not being done, and the social costs of such neglect can be high. Similarly, feelings of anxiety signal to you the need to be vigilant against threats, and feelings of jealousy signal the need to pay attention to relationships that you may have taken for granted. In each case, an accurate recognition of what you are feeling is necessary so that you can focus on the right thing, and then take corrective actions.

Emotions provide further benefits

The third reason why an accurate recognition of your own moods is important is that having this kind of knowledge about internal states can lead to other beneficial outcomes. For example, research suggests that people who have the most clarity regarding their emotional states tend to be less depressed, and to generally experience less emotional distress, than those who have less understanding of their moods.

Other research suggests that during times of high stress and arousal, those with clearer recognition of their emotional states actually perform better. One study examined firefighters who were undergoing highly realistic training inside heat- and smoke-filled buildings; those who had previously scored higher on a measure that taps how clearly emotions are experienced reported that they were better able to think clearly in those extreme settings, and were less likely to "blank out" and forget their training, than those whose scores were lower. In a variety of ways, therefore, having accurate knowledge about your own internal states is a highly desirable state of affairs.

Recognition of emotional states in others

While it may at first seem a little odd to speak of difficulties in recognizing your own emotional states, it does not seem at all strange to speak of difficulties in identifying emotions in others. Other people can be frustratingly difficult to "read," often at times when you most want to be able to read them (at the poker table; on a first date); difficulties in understanding what someone is "really" feeling are sadly all too common. Moreover, as important as it can be to accurately identify your own emotional states, it is probably just as important to correctly recognize emotions in others. Again, there are many reasons for this, but let me emphasize two.

Emotions are information

Just as your own emotions signal to you what you value highly and what you value not at all, the emotional states of other people convey similar information about *their* likes and dislikes. An accurate appraisal of others' emotions therefore provides you with valid information; an inaccurate estimate of others' emotions provides you with useless, or even misleading, information.

When you think of it, social life is chock-full of opportunities for you to misjudge the emotion that another person is feeling ("My wife must have been thrilled when I gave her that new garden hose for our tenth wedding anniversary. Did you see the way her face reddened and her eyes brimmed with tears?"). The fewer of those opportunities you take, the smoother and more pleasant your social life is likely to be.

Emotions are useful for the pursuit of your goals

An accurate recognition of others' emotions is useful to you in the pursuit of your goals. This can unfold in a variety of ways. At the most basic level it may occur during one-on-one encounters with others. For example, consider a doctor who is treating a patient. In addition to noting objective facts such as blood pressure, heart rate, lab results and so on, the doctor tries to assess the patient's emotional state. Is he worried? Is he *extremely* worried? Is he in pain? Is he hiding his emotional state? An accurate assessment of the patient's mood may be even more important if the doctor must deliver a distressing diagnosis. How much bad news can the patient absorb? How much time should the doctor spend with him? Is follow-up counseling necessary? In order for the doctor to effectively serve the patient, an accurate recognition of the patient's emotional state may be critical. Errors in emotion recognition could mean an inaccurate diagnosis or needless stress, or might lead to a patient being resistant to recommended treatment. The stakes could be very high indeed.

As another example, consider a saleswoman attempting to convince a potential customer of the value of her product (let's say, a new line of full-body toupees for cats). Assessing the customer's mood state can be an important component of the persuasion effort. Is he cheerful? Annoyed? Willing to listen to more testimonials about the superiority of her product? Laughing too hard to listen to the sales pitch? All salespeople are ultimately in the business of persuasion, and the mood of the audience is always an important factor during persuasion attempts. In fact, it is difficult to think of any occupations in which it is *not* useful to have a good ability to accurately recognize the emotional states of others.

The usefulness of emotional recognition is not limited to one-on-one encounters. An ability to correctly recognize others' emotions also provides useful information about the more general "social terrain." That is, just as it is useful to know any individual's mood state, knowing something about the larger social network is also helpful. For example, a newcomer to an organization quickly tries to learn who the major players are, and how they are linked to each other emotionally. Who likes whom? Who are the boss's favorites? Who is genuinely popular, and who is merely tolerated? What are the important social cliques? Although there is more than one way to acquire such information, one fundamental method of doing so is by observing social encounters and making an accurate assessment of what people are genuinely feeling as they interact with each other.

Methods of estimating emotional states

It is clear that being able to correctly perceive and recognize emotions has a profound value. But how can you accomplish this? That is, how do you go about making estimates of emotional states? In the case of your own emotions, a big part of success at this task seems to be simple attention. For most of us the most formidable obstacle to recognizing our own emotions is that we never stop to pay attention to them.

Emotions may be a kind of information, but it is

information that is not communicated to you through the familiar channel of language. Instead, information about your emotions is conveyed to you through sweaty palms, changes in heart rate, tensed muscles and a host of other signals from the body. Perhaps the single biggest factor in accurately perceiving your own emotions is a willingness to stop directing all of your attention outwards toward the world and instead to sometimes direct it inwards, so that you become aware of these messages from your flesh and bones. Chapter 6 presents some techniques for improving your ability to focus attention on your internal states, and thus your ability to recognize your emotions and moods.

While attention alone may be sufficient for recognizing your own feelings, the process is more complicated when you attempt to determine the emotions of others. The task now is more difficult: you must use something *visible* (others' behavior and appearance) to infer something *invisible* (what they are feeling). One important way in which this is done—perhaps the major way—is through the interpretation of other people's faces. Psychologists have spent decades studying facial expressions, the link between facial expressions and emotions, and our ability to infer emotional states from facial information. This research has led to at least four conclusions:

1. There appears to be a relatively small number of primary emotions that are associated with particular

facial expressions. Most investigators agree on six or seven such emotions: fear, anger, happiness, surprise, sadness, disgust and (possibly) contempt. (Of course, there are many more emotions possible, including blends of these particular ones.)

2. People around the world tend to use the same facial expressions when experiencing these emotions. Evidence from a number of cross-cultural investigations supports the conclusion that these six or seven combinations of emotions and facial expressions are universal; the same combinations occur in London, Moscow and isolated parts of New Guinea.

3. People are reasonably accurate at judging emotion from faces, although we tend to do best when judging members of our own culture.

4. Although accuracy in inferring emotions is generally good, there are nevertheless stable differences between people in their ability to do this kind of judging.

Facial information is not the only method available for detecting others' moods. Although not as extensive, research has also examined our ability to use other kinds of information for this task: the target's voice, posture, physical movements and so on. It is fair to say, however, that facial information has a special importance when we try to infer another's emotions.

TESTS

As mentioned in chapter 1 (see page 12), most of the components of EQ are measured in this book in multiple ways—through some combination of self-report, multirater and performance tests. This strategy helps to provide a reasonably reliable way for you to evaluate your standing in each area. The one exception to this pattern is the very first EQ component we consider: recognizing your own emotions. This dimension is assessed here by only a single, self-report test.

The reason for this is that this particular dimension of EQ is quite difficult to assess in any other way. A multirater test is not appropriate in this case, because asking *other* people how well you recognize your own emotions is very difficult for them: how would they *know* if you accurately recognize your feelings? A performance test is also inappropriate, again because of difficulties in scoring. If a test taker claims to experience a particular emotion, how can the test tell him he's wrong?

This chapter therefore concludes with three tests:

- One test to measure the ability to recognize your own emotions (self-report test).
- Two tests to assess the ability to recognize the emotions of others (self-report and multirater tests).

For these tests, and all the others in this book, consult the section "Scoring and interpreting your EQ tests" (see page 162) for detailed instructions on how to calculate and interpret your scores.

Test Your EQ

TEST 1

Recognizing your own emotions
Self-report test

Indicate how well each of the following statements describes you. Be as frank and honest as possible; the test can only be useful if your answers are accurate. In responding to each item, use one of the following choices:

1 = This is **never** true of me
2 = This is **rarely** true of me
3 = This is **sometimes** true of me
4 = This is **frequently** true of me
5 = This is **always** true of me

☐ 1. I know exactly what I'm feeling.

☐ 2. I cannot accurately describe my emotional state to other people.

☐ 3. I am highly aware of changes in my mood.

☐ 4. In emotional situations, I notice changes in my body.

☐ 5. I can tell when I start to feel frustrated or angry.

30

☐ 6. Other people notice changes in my mood before I do.

☐ 7. I pay little attention to my internal states (thoughts and feelings).

☐ 8. I am in touch with my feelings.

☐ 9. I am surprised by the emotional reactions that I have.

☐ 10. I find it difficult to put my feelings into words.

TEST 2

Recognizing emotions in others
Self-report test

Indicate how well each of the following statements describes you. Be as frank and honest as possible in your answers; this test can only be useful if your answers are accurate. In responding to each item, use one of the following choices:

1 = This is **never** true of me
2 = This is **rarely** true of me
3 = This is **sometimes** true of me
4 = This is **frequently** true of me
5 = This is **always** true of me

1. I recognize when someone else is becoming angry.

2. I recognize when a coworker is sad or depressed.

3. I have no clue as to what other people are feeling.

4. I misread what is happening in emotional situations.

5. I pay a lot of attention to other people's emotional states.

6. I am skilled at recognizing other people's emotions.

7. When a friend is feeling lots of stress, I am slow to notice.

☐ 8. Other people's emotions are difficult to recognize.

☐ 9. When I am part of a group of people, I am sensitive to the emotional "climate" among them.

☐ 10. I am slow to notice when the boss is in an especially good mood.

TEST 3

Recognizing emotions in others
Multirater test

At least one person who knows you well should complete this test, answering the questions about you. It is even better if several people complete the test, so that you can get a broader picture of how others view your EQ abilities. Once they have done so, you can score the tests using the instructions provided (see page 169).

Indicate how well each of the following statements describes the person you are being asked to rate. Be as frank and honest as possible in your answers; this test can only be useful if your answers are accurate. In responding to each item, use one of the following choices:

1 = This is **never** true of the person
2 = This is **rarely** true of the person
3 = This is **sometimes** true of the person
4 = This is **frequently** true of the person
5 = This is **always** true of the person

1. This person recognizes when someone is becoming angry.

2. This person is good at recognizing the emotions of others.

3. This person does not realize it when other people are bored or uninterested.

4. This person notices when a coworker is sad or depressed.

5. This person totally misreads what is happening in emotional situations.

6. This person is aware of the emotional states of friends and family members.

7. This person is slow to notice when the boss is in an especially good mood.

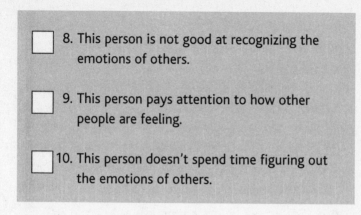

☐ 8. This person is not good at recognizing the emotions of others.

☐ 9. This person pays attention to how other people are feeling.

☐ 10. This person doesn't spend time figuring out the emotions of others.

3
UNDERSTANDING EMOTIONS

THE SECOND SKILL contributing to emotional intelligence is the *ability to understand emotions*. This component goes beyond the fundamental ability simply to recognize emotional states; now the focus is on having some meaningful knowledge about emotions. Again, this can refer to an understanding of either our own emotions or those of other people.

Obviously, a thorough understanding of emotions— their causes, their consequences, how they develop and change over time—is crucial, as we try to use emotions in order to function effectively in the world. If the ability to recognize emotions can be likened to learning the alphabet, then understanding emotions may be compared to understanding how language works—the meanings of words, how sentences are constructed, the differences between nouns and verbs, and everything else that contributes to our ability to communicate.

So what does it mean to say that we "understand" emotions? Again, there are multiple ways to answer this question, but let me focus on three different aspects of emotion that psychologists have considered as they have tried to sort out this aspect of emotional intelligence.

Understanding the causes of emotions

The first important thing to understand about emotions is what causes them. For example, once you recognize an emotion you are feeling, the next question is *"Why* am I feeling this way?" In some ways, the answer to this question is as important as (or more important than) the recognition of the emotion itself.

Let us return for a moment to an example mentioned in the previous chapter: a woman is interviewing job applicants and becomes aware of some negative feelings while interviewing one particular applicant. That feeling provides some information to the interviewer, but what does the information mean? The feeling might be the result of something superficial and unimportant—perhaps the applicant bears a slight physical resemblance to a loutish ex-husband. On the other hand, the uneasiness could be the result of something more important—the interviewer may be responding to nonverbal cues from the applicant indicating boredom, irritation or lack

37

of respect for the interviewer. Understanding the cause of this feeling, then, is crucial: in the first instance, the feeling is really irrelevant to how the applicant is likely to perform if hired and should probably be ignored; in the second, the feeling might well be an indicator of trouble ahead, and thus may have a legitimate place in the hiring decision.

Understanding the causes of emotions is valuable not only when the emotions are your own, but also when they are being felt by other people. Thus, although it is important to accurately recognize the emotion your spouse is experiencing at the dinner table (anger, not delight), it can be even more important to know *why* that feeling exists. Is he angry because his boss is making unreasonable demands at work? Because the car is acting up again? Or because of something *you* have said, done, failed to say or failed to do? An incorrect answer to this question will obviously influence how this particular occasion will unfold. However, a more *general* inability to answer such questions may have repercussions that go far beyond this particular evening.

Understanding the consequences of emotions

The next important thing to understand about emotions is the effect they have: in short, the consequences of emotions. Just as it is important to know where emotions come from, it is also important to know how they influence the person who experiences them. For example, consider a teacher who arrives home one evening in a foul mood: the traffic was terrible, the weather is miserable and the Cubs have lost three in a row. Being in an angry mood (even for reasons as good as these!) has some predictable and generally undesirable effects on behavior; among other things, anger can make us more short-tempered and less forgiving of others.

If the teacher has a good understanding of emotional consequences, he may decide that this is not a good night to read and grade his students' essays; at the very least he will be especially alert to the possibility that his judgments tonight may be unnecessarily harsh. If, however, the teacher does not have a good understanding of emotional consequences, he might instead spend the evening marking papers and becoming increasingly infuriated by the unusually poor quality of his students' work. The advantage of accurate emotional understanding in this case is that it helps prevent a temporary emotional state from having an unwanted and unwarranted effect on behavior.

It can be similarly valuable to have an understanding of emotional consequences when the emotions are those of other people. To take an obvious case, knowing how your boss acts when he is in an angry mood can allow you to avoid him, placate him or in some other way try to minimize the negative effects (on you!) of the boss's temporary mood.

The consequences of emotions can also be more

subtle. For instance, knowing that a friend has been passed over for promotion will probably lead you to accurately perceive that she is feeling resentment; but what effect will that have on her behavior? One possibility is that her resentment will lead her to become less committed to her job and less reliable in carrying out her responsibilities. Her work may start to contain a few more errors, and she may miss a few deadlines. These are behaviors that are not nearly as dramatic as the emotional outbursts of an angry boss, and might not even be noticed by most people, at least not at first; for someone with a good understanding of emotional consequences, however, these behavioral reactions are perfectly predictable and recognizable.

The importance of perspective taking

Before turning to the third important thing to understand about emotions, let us pause for a bit and consider more deeply the process by which you come to understand the emotions of other people—how you come to determine the causes and effects of their feelings.

In chapter 2 I made the argument that a basic method for recognizing your own emotional state is to focus attention inwards so as to better notice the changes that emotions produce in you. To more accurately understand emotions in others—both their causes and consequences—you need to have the ability and willingness to look *outside* yourself as well. In particular, to have the best understanding of how emotions will affect other people, you need to be able to see things from their perspective—to imagine what they are feeling and thinking. In short, being able and willing to empathize with other people should be extremely helpful to deepening your understanding of their emotions.

How exactly might this work? That is, how does taking the perspective of others actually produce increased understanding of them? To answer that, let's take as an example a very common psychological finding: the fact that people tend to explain their own actions somewhat differently from the way that outside observers do. In brief, what this means is that we tend to see our own behavior as resulting more from external factors than from our internal characteristics; observers tend to do the reverse, usually explaining our behavior as more due to our own traits and dispositions.

As an example, I am likely to explain why I was late for work today in terms of external forces—my alarm clock did not go off, the traffic was horrible, my car was full of bees again and so on. In contrast, a coworker is more likely to explain my behavior in terms of something internal to me—laziness, irresponsibility or being disorganized. This very reliable phenomenon indicates that observers are usually somewhat inaccurate when trying to imagine how another person views the world— my coworkers do not recognize the external factors that I blame for my behavior because they are focusing on internal ones. Interestingly, however, when observers are prompted to imagine the point of view of the other person—to actually engage in perspective taking—they begin to explain the other's behavior in more situational terms. In short, taking the other's perspective reliably leads observers to see the world in the way in which the other person does.

It is in this way that perspective taking can help you have a better understanding of another's emotions. If your boss is in a touchy mood, for example, a good way to predict the consequences of this is to imagine how the world now looks to her. How would *you* feel if you were already irritated and an employee asked for help? Happy to offer assistance to another living creature, or increasingly angered by a needy and lazy subordinate? The key to successfully understanding emotional consequences in this case lies in seeing the innocent request for help not through your own eyes, but through the jaundiced viewpoint of the other person—in a word, through perspective taking.

Understanding how emotions work

The third important thing to understand regarding emotions is not so much concerned with causes and consequences in particular cases; it is more about possessing a *general understanding of how emotions work.* For example, in addition to being able to discern exactly why the boss is in a foul mood today, it is also valuable to possess a more general understanding of the regular and predictable factors that *usually* contribute to emotional responses. This would include information such as "joy often results from unexpected good fortune," and "the inexplicable success of a rival often produces envy." In a way, this kind of ability is more about having a "theory" of emotions in general and less about specific cases. Possessing this kind of general understanding of emotions can be especially helpful when you are faced with new situations involving people with whom you may not be familiar.

To develop this theme further, one somewhat surprising finding from social psychology in recent years is that people are generally not able to predict how strongly an emotional event will affect them. For instance, if we are asked to estimate how strong our positive emotions would be, or how long they would last, if we were to win a $10 million lottery, most of us tend to *over*estimate both of those judgments. We tend to imagine that our joy will be more intense than it actually turns out to be, and that this feeling will persist for substantially longer than it actually does. The same overestimates occur when we try to predict our reactions to negative events. One implication of this tendency is therefore that we are often prone to make decisions based on faulty assumptions—in particular, the assumption that bad events will make us feel worse and feel worse longer than would actually be the case.

Consider a middle-aged psychologist who is considering an unpleasant but recommended medical procedure (let's say a colonoscopy to screen for cancer). He might well imagine that the discomfort and embarrassment associated with the procedure will be worse than it really will be, and that these unpleasant feelings will last longer than they actually will; in fact, his overestimates may lead him to not have the procedure done at all. Had our hypothetical psychologist possessed a better understanding of how emotions work—especially an implicit understanding that emotions fade faster than we might expect—this might have helped him make a wiser long-term decision.

There are several emotion-related insights of this type—knowledge, either conscious or nonconscious, about how emotions really work. Having some meaningful understanding of these "mechanisms" of emotion is a potentially important element of this aspect of EQ.

Putting it all together

When these three forms of emotional understanding are combined, a powerful mixture results. People who understand emotional causes, emotional consequences and how emotions work generally are able to see the "big picture" more clearly than those who do not have such understanding. For example, one very important advantage these people have is that they are better able to anticipate how their own behavior—even the most trivial—might influence the emotional reactions of those around them. For instance, we all sometimes have to make unpopular decisions, and these decisions can often lead to disappointment in others; having a sophisticated understanding of emotional causes and consequences can make us more careful about *how* unpopular decisions are made and communicated.

Delivering the bad news in a blunt, no-nonsense fashion can create considerably more anger and resentment than the decision alone would ordinarily produce. Delivering the same bad news in a different way—one that explains the decision-making process, and makes clear that the decision is painful to us as well—can often drastically reduce the intensity of the resentment. Perspective taking (see page 40) can be particularly helpful in such cases, allowing us to imagine how our words and actions might be interpreted.

Seeing the emotional big picture can be especially useful in organizational contexts—when there are more than one or two individuals involved, the emotional landscape can become complicated, and a thorough understanding of emotional processes may be necessary in order to see what that landscape is really like.

An ability to see the big picture can, for example, help us to figure out what the most important issues and values are for an organization. It will lead us to ask some important questions, such as:

- What are the issues that seem to arouse the strongest emotional response in the people working for the organization?

- What (if anything) do those issues have in common?
- Are the same issues important to both the organization's leaders and the rank and file?
- What do the emotional responses of these people reveal about the relevant cliques and social groups within the organization?

As we have seen before, emotion is information, but the information means more to people who understand it most thoroughly. Having this kind of understanding is a powerful tool.

TESTS

This chapter concludes with nine tests designed to measure four aspects of emotional understanding:

- Two tests tap your ability to understand the causes of your own emotions (self-report and performance tests).
- Two tests tap your ability to understand the causes of others' emotions (self-report and multirater tests).
- Two tests measure the ability to understand the consequences of your own emotions (self-report and performance tests).
- Three tests measure your ability to understand the consequences of emotions in others (self-report, multirater and performance tests).

TEST 4

Understanding the causes of your own emotions
Self-report test

Indicate how well each of the following statements describes you. Be as frank and honest as possible in your answers; this test can only be useful if your answers are accurate. In responding to each item, use one of the following choices:

1 = This is **never** true of me
2 = This is **rarely** true of me
3 = This is **sometimes** true of me
4 = This is **frequently** true of me
5 = This is **always** true of me

☐ 1. When I feel sad or depressed, I am able to figure out what is causing it.

☐ 2. I have a keen understanding of what causes my moods.

☐ 3. My moods are predictable and understandable.

☐ 4. I am confused as to why I am feeling what I'm feeling.

☐ 5. I don't have very good insight into what causes my moods.

☐ 6. I can figure out the reason for my emotions.

☐ 7. When I feel anxious I can't put into words why I feel that way.

☐ 8. My moods change and I'm not sure why.

☐ 9. I like to figure out the reasons for why I feel the way I do.

☐ 10. I don't spend much time trying to figure out what causes my moods.

TEST 5

Understanding the causes of your own emotions
Performance test

Each of the following items describes a social situation in which you might find yourself. After each description you will be asked to indicate the *most likely* emotional response—or responses—that *you personally* would experience. In some cases only one emotional response is likely; in others there will be more than one. Circle all the

responses that you think would be *likely*—not just theoretically possible—in that situation.

1. It is the end of the year and your boss has
   informed everyone about salaries for next
   year. You and your best friend at work tell
   each other what you will earn. You have
   received a healthy pay increase but your
   friend received no increase at all. Which of
   the following are likely emotional responses
   that you will feel?

   a. Happiness
   b. Embarrassment
   c. Guilt
   d. Anger

2. You spend several hours preparing a special
   birthday meal for your spouse. Afterward, he
   or she gives you a peck on the cheek and
   says thanks. Which of the following are likely
   emotional responses that you will feel?

   a. Irritation
   b. Pride
   c. Guilt
   d. Disappointment

3. At work, your boss singles you out during a meeting as the person who is doing the best work in the office, and says that the others should be more like you. Which of the following are likely emotional responses that you will feel?

   a. Anger
   b. Amusement
   c. Pride
   d. Embarrassment

4. On the day that you have to give an important presentation at work, you have a loud argument with your daughter just before you leave the house. As you drive to work, which of the following are likely emotional responses that you will feel?

   a. Calmness
   b. Nervousness
   c. Anger
   d. Amusement

5. You are selling your house, and have just received an offer from a potential buyer. The offer is for the full amount that you are

asking, but it also requires that you repaint the exterior, which you did not plan to do. Which of the following are likely emotional responses that you will feel?

a. Resentment
b. Happiness
c. Amusement
d. Fear

6. One week after your best friend was diagnosed with a life-threatening illness, you are told that you have received an important promotion. Your first major responsibility will be a presentation to upper management in three days. Which of the following are likely emotional responses that you will feel?

a. Depression
b. Anxiety
c. Pride
d. Embarrassment

7. A day after eating at an expensive restaurant, you notice on your credit card receipt that the waitress undercharged you by $30. Which of the following are likely emotional responses that you will feel?

a. Irritation
b. Depression
c. Guilt
d. Pleasure

8. You are at a party where loud music is playing. You are telling a mildly off-color joke to a friend, but just as you deliver the risque punchline, the music stops and everyone can hear you. Which of the following are likely emotional responses that you will feel?

a. Amusement
b. Anger
c. Fear
d. Embarrassment

9. Despite your many warnings never to touch a very expensive and very sharp knife, your seven-year-old son has used it while making you a birthday present. Which of the following are likely emotional responses that you will feel?

a. Anger
b. Resentment

c. Amusement

d. Forgiveness

10. Your boss has decided to give you and your work group some important new responsibilities. It is a substantial honor, but will also require that you work longer hours, including evenings and weekends. As you prepare to tell your spouse about the news, which of the following are likely emotional responses that you will feel?

a. Pride

b. Apprehension

c. Amusement

d. Embarrassment

TEST 6

Understanding the causes of others' emotions
Self-report test

Indicate how well each of the following statements describes you. Be as frank and honest as possible in your answers; this test can only be useful if your answers are accurate. In responding to each item, use one of the following choices:

1 = This is **never** true of me
2 = This is **rarely** true of me
3 = This is **sometimes** true of me
4 = This is **frequently** true of me
5 = This is **always** true of me

☐ 1. When someone else is feeling depressed I can figure out why.

☐ 2. When someone else is irritated or angry I have difficulty understanding the reason.

☐ 3. I am able to understand the causes of others' emotions.

☐ 4. It's hard for me to figure out why people experience the moods that they do.

☐ 5. When people get irritated with me I really don't know why.

☐ 6. I'm good at explaining why my friends feel the way they do.

☐ 7. When my spouse seems worried or upset I can figure out why.

8. My boss's moods are hard for me to understand.

9. I can diagnose the causes of people's emotional states.

10. I don't spend time and effort trying to determine why other people feel the way they do.

TEST 7

Understanding the causes of others' emotions
Multirater test

At least one person who knows you well should complete this test, answering the questions about you. It is even better if several people complete the test, so that you can get a broader picture of how others view your EQ abilities. Once they have done so, you can score the tests using the instructions provided (see page 170).

Indicate how well each of the following statements describes the person you are being asked to rate. Be as frank and honest as possible in your answers; this test can only be useful if your answers are accurate. In responding to each item, use one of the following choices:

1 = This is **never** true of the person
2 = This is **rarely** true of the person
3 = This is **sometimes** true of the person
4 = This is **frequently** true of the person
5 = This is **always** true of the person

☐ 1. This person is good at understanding the reasons behind other people's emotions.

☐ 2. This person can figure out why someone is depressed.

☐ 3. This person has difficulty understanding the complicated causes of others' emotions.

☐ 4. This person is not able to explain why coworkers feel the way they do.

☐ 5. This person can't tell why another person is angry.

☐ 6. This person is skilled at figuring out why someone's mood has changed.

☐ 7. This person is not good at determining why someone else is in a good mood.

8. This person understands even the very subtle causes of emotions in other people.

9. This person has difficulty understanding why other people become jealous.

10. This person tries hard to understand what is causing their friends' emotions.

TEST 8

***Understanding the consequences of your own emotions
Self-report test***

Indicate how well each of the following statements describes you. Be as frank and honest as possible in your answers; this test can only be useful if your answers are accurate. In responding to each item, use one of the following choices:

1 = This is **never** true of me
2 = This is **rarely** true of me
3 = This is **sometimes** true of me
4 = This is **frequently** true of me
5 = This is **always** true of me

☐ 1. My emotions have predictable effects on how I act toward others.

☐ 2. When I am feeling anxious, I have a good idea of the effect this will have on my performance.

☐ 3. I have a solid understanding of how my emotions affect my behavior.

☐ 4. When I'm in a bad mood I don't know what effect it will have on me.

☐ 5. When I'm feeling lots of frustration, my behavior is easy to predict.

☐ 6. Even when I am feeling a very clear emotion, I am uncertain what will come next.

☐ 7. Being in a good mood has little effect on my judgment and behavior.

☐ 8. If I start the day in a bad mood, I can predict how the rest of the day will go.

☐ 9. I don't have much understanding of how my emotions affect my behavior.

10. When my anger flares up, the effect it has on my behavior is unpredictable.

TEST 9

Understanding the consequences of your own emotions
Performance test

Each of the following questions describes a social situation in which you might find yourself. After each description you will be asked to indicate the *most likely* emotional response—or responses—that *you personally* would experience. In some cases only one emotional response is likely; in others there will be more than one. Circle all the responses that you think would be *likely*—not just theoretically possible—in that situation.

1. You have been feeling sad and depressed for some time. Which of the following are likely effects on your behavior?

   a. Loss of appetite
   b. Inability to sleep
   c. Improvement in concentration
   d. Loss of interest in sex

2. You have been experiencing heightened anxiety for several days. Which of the following are likely effects on your behavior?

   a. Increase in appetite
   b. Increase in optimism
   c. Difficulty sleeping
   d. "Butterflies in your stomach"

3. You are experiencing anger toward a member of your family. Which of the following are likely effects on your behavior?

   a. Feeling of calm well-being
   b. Irritation at other people
   c. Frequent thoughts about that person
   d. Greater productivity at work

4. You are embarrassed about a simple mistake that you made at work. Which of the following are likely effects on your behavior?

   a. Become more introverted
   b. Increase in confidence

    c. Improvement in concentration
    d. Lowering of self-esteem

5. You are in a great mood. Which of the following are likely effects on your behavior?

    a. Become more talkative
    b. Improvement in concentration
    c. Become more short-tempered
    d. Become more generous

6. You are feeling a lot of pride because of your daughter's accomplishments at school. Which of the following are likely effects on your behavior?

    a. Become more short-tempered
    b. Loss of appetite
    c. Lowering of self-esteem
    d. Tell others about her accomplishments

7. You are feeling quite envious of a coworker who got a promotion that you felt you deserved. Which of the following are likely effects on your behavior?

a. Difficulties in concentration
b. Become more generous
c. Greater productivity at work
d. Become more self-centered

8. You are feeling resentful toward your boss, who has required you to work late every night for a week. Which of the following are likely effects on your behavior?

a. Become sarcastic toward boss
b. Complain to coworkers
c. Feel proud that the boss relies on you
d. Become jealous of coworkers

9. You are somewhat infatuated with a new person in your social circle. Which of the following are likely effects on your behavior?

a. Laugh more readily at this person's jokes
b. Become more concerned about your appearance
c. Lowering of self-esteem
d. Become more irritable

10. You are feeling guilty because of a rude comment you made about an acquaintance. Which of the following are likely effects on your behavior?

   a. Avoid the person
   b. Become depressed
   c. Feelings of calm satisfaction
   d. Do something nice for the person

TEST 10

Understanding the consequences of others' emotions
Self-report test

Indicate how well each of the following statements describes you. Be as frank and honest as possible in your answers; this test can only be useful if your answers are accurate. In responding to each item, use one of the following choices:

1 = This is **never** true of me
2 = This is **rarely** true of me
3 = This is **sometimes** true of me
4 = This is **frequently** true of me
5 = This is **always** true of me

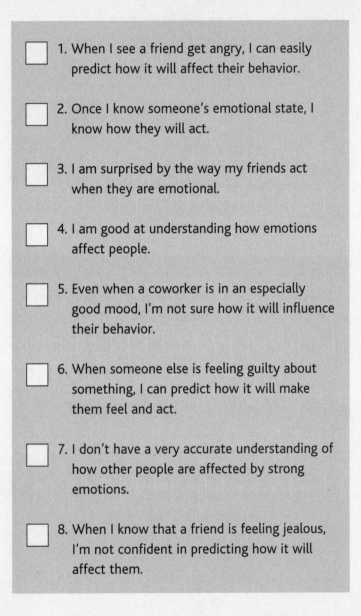

☐ 1. When I see a friend get angry, I can easily predict how it will affect their behavior.

☐ 2. Once I know someone's emotional state, I know how they will act.

☐ 3. I am surprised by the way my friends act when they are emotional.

☐ 4. I am good at understanding how emotions affect people.

☐ 5. Even when a coworker is in an especially good mood, I'm not sure how it will influence their behavior.

☐ 6. When someone else is feeling guilty about something, I can predict how it will make them feel and act.

☐ 7. I don't have a very accurate understanding of how other people are affected by strong emotions.

☐ 8. When I know that a friend is feeling jealous, I'm not confident in predicting how it will affect them.

☐ 9. I can tell how someone's mood will affect their thoughts and actions.

☐ 10. I don't think much about how others' emotions will affect them.

Understanding the consequences of others' emotions
Multirater test

At least one person who knows you well should complete this test, answering the questions about you. It is even better if several people complete the test, so that you can get a broader picture of how others view your EQ abilities. Once they have done so, you can score the tests using the instructions provided (see page 170).

Indicate how well each of the following statements describes the person you are being asked to rate. Be as frank and honest as possible in your answers; this test can only be useful if your answers are accurate. In responding to each item, use one of the following choices:

1 = This is **never** true of the person
2 = This is **rarely** true of the person
3 = This is **sometimes** true of the person
4 = This is **frequently** true of the person
5 = This is **always** true of the person

☐ 1. This person understands the effects of moods on others' behavior.

☐ 2. This person understands how a depressed person is likely to feel and act.

☐ 3. This person is not good when it comes to predicting someone's behavior from their emotions.

☐ 4. This person does not understand how another person's anger can influence their actions.

☐ 5. This person has difficulty in understanding how others act as a result of their emotional states.

☐ 6. This person understands the link between someone's emotions and their behavior.

☐ 7. This person is not skillful at figuring out how strong emotions affect people.

☐ 8. This person can determine how their friends' moods will influence their friends' behavior.

9. This person is at a loss when trying to understand the connection between others' emotions and their actions.

10. This person makes an effort to understand how their friends' emotions influence their behavior.

TEST 12

Understanding the consequences of others' emotions
Performance test

Each of the following questions describes a situation in which someone you know is experiencing an emotion. After each description you are asked to indicate the *most likely* effect—or effects—that the emotion would have *on that person*. In some cases only one effect is likely; in others there will be more than one. Circle all the effects that you think would be *likely*—not just theoretically possible—in that situation.

1. You have a friend who has been feeling a lot of anger toward her brother. Which of the following are likely effects on her behavior?

a. Increased optimism
b. Fewer interactions with her brother
c. Increased irritability
d. Better performance at work

2. Your boss has been in a good mood all week. Which of the following are likely effects on her behavior? She is:

a. More likely to agree to give you a pay raise
b. More critical of mistakes by staff
c. More tolerant of people leaving early
d. Less demanding

3. Your friend is depressed because his girlfriend has left him. Which of the following are likely effects on his behavior?

a. Difficulties in sleeping
b. Increased energy
c. Increased appetite
d. Difficulty in concentrating

4. A coworker is feeling very grateful toward you because you have helped him with an important project. Which of the following are likely effects on his behavior? He is:

    a. Likely to make less eye contact with you
    b. More critical of you
    c. More considerate of you
    d. Beginning to avoid you

5. Your spouse is feeling jealous of a colleague at work who is a favorite of the boss. Which of the following are likely effects on your spouse's behavior? He or she becomes more:

    a. Critical of the boss
    b. Generous to the coworker
    c. Calm and even-tempered
    d. Sarcastic about the coworker

6. Your teenage son is feeling embarrassed because of his physical awkwardness and recent voice change. Which of the following are likely effects on his behavior? He becomes more:

    a. Even-tempered
    b. Self-critical
    c. Anxious around people
    d. Self-confident

7. A colleague at work is feeling insecure because she is not sure she deserves her new job and the responsibilities that go with it. Which of the following are likely effects on her behavior? She becomes:

   a. More hesitant before making decisions
   b. More critical of her staff
   c. Less willing to admit error
   d. More complimentary to her staff

8. A coworker is bitter because he feels he is not appreciated by the organization. Which of the following are likely effects on his behavior? He:

   a. Works harder than ever
   b. Begins to slack off at work
   c. Criticizes the organization to other people
   d. Withdraws from coworkers

9. You have a coworker who is bored with her job. Which of the following are likely effects on her behavior? She:

   a. Begins to slack off at work
   b. Begins to criticize the organization

    c. Spends extra time working nights and weekends

    d. Withdraws from coworkers

10. Your boss is very ambitious and eager to be promoted to a higher position in the organization. Which of the following are likely effects on his behavior? He:

    a. Spends lots of extra time at work

    b. Volunteers your department for special tasks

    c. Avoids contact with those in senior management

    d. Shares credit with all members of your department

4
REGULATING AND CONTROLLING EMOTIONS

THUS FAR, THE emotional intelligence skills we have been discussing have had a somewhat "passive" quality to them. That is, the skills of recognizing and understanding emotions, as important as they are, do not typically require us to *do* anything with the emotions in question. This is not to say that recognizing and understanding emotions requires no effort, but these skills are essentially about *reacting* in some way to the emotions that we encounter in our lives.

The third skill contributing to emotional intelligence— *the ability to regulate and control emotion*—goes beyond the relatively passive skills discussed thus far.

With the introduction of this EQ skill, you will begin to see that you can do more than recognize emotions and know how they work; you can also to a considerable degree manipulate and control the emotions you encounter around you.

This is an important turning point in our discussion. The ability to regulate emotions allows you an enormous flexibility in your emotional and social lives. Instead of being forced to accept the emotional "cards"dealt to you, you can actively try to change those cards. As a result, the ability to successfully control emotions leads directly to a number of highly important and beneficial outcomes. Some of these outcomes result from your ability to regulate your own emotions, others from your ability to regulate the emotions of others. Let us therefore consider each of these possibilities separately.

Regulating our own emotions

In many ways, the mark of mature individuals is their ability to master themselves—to control their desires, wishes, impulses and emotions rather than be controlled by them. People who lack this ability are often described in some pretty uncomplimentary ways: immature, impulsive, irrational, shortsighted and childish, to name a few. To be sure, some situations can be so powerful or dramatic that any of us might be temporarily overcome by emotion. For emotionally intelligent people, however, this is a relatively uncommon occurrence; most of the time they are able to regulate their feelings well enough to retain self-control. Such control leads directly to a number of important benefits.

Controlling arousal levels to maximize performance

The first of these benefits is perhaps the most obvious one: an ability to regulate your emotions allows you to control arousal levels so as to maximize your performance. It has long been known that arousal has a predictable, U-shaped relationship with performance. Performance tends to be poor when there are very low levels of arousal and very high levels of arousal; the best performance is typically at intermediate arousal levels. In most situations requiring emotional regulation, of course, the problem is not too *little* arousal, but too much.

It is easy to think of dramatic cases where it is critically important to control your emotional arousal. Soldiers in combat must not allow their very high levels of arousal to prevent them from carrying out their mission; air-traffic controllers must not allow their arousal levels during a crisis to interfere with making split-second life-or-death decisions; the parents of a seriously injured child must not let their fear turn into panic and prevent them from taking the steps necessary to get the proper medical attention. Even in less dramatic settings, though, you are frequently faced with the need to somehow control your emotions so as to prevent arousal levels from getting too high. Taking an important examination at school, making a crucial presentation at work or trying to impress a prospective employer are also situations in which the ability to think clearly and perform effectively can be undermined if arousal levels are not moderated.

Persisting despite frustration and temptation
Another benefit of being able to regulate your own emotions is that it allows you to persist in the face of frustration and temptation. One of the things that can sabotage even your most well-intentioned goals is the presence of a strong competing emotion. For example, you may have firm intentions to stick to your diet, but the unexpected presence of a freshly baked cinnamon bun—still warm from the oven, covered with a white sugary glaze, wafting a sweet fragrance as you gaze at its moist softness—can be, well, distracting! The competing emotion in this case is a desire for the tasty snack. If powerful enough, a competing emotion can lead you to abandon a strongly held goal for a brief (if delightful) moment of pleasure.

Sometimes the competing emotion is not so much a desire for something attractive, but a desire to stop doing something that is not intrinsically interesting. A regular exercise regimen can be an important goal for reasons both medical and aesthetic, but for many people the act of exercising is not intrinsically interesting. It is not fun. It is, in a word, boring. The competing emotion in this case is a desire to do something—anything—other than exercise, and if that feeling is not controlled it can put an end to the exercise program. The large number of stationary bicycles and treadmills gathering dust and cobwebs in bedrooms and basements is a monument to the difficulty of this kind of emotional regulation.

In both these examples, the ability to regulate emotions is necessary in order to persist in a desired course of action. In one case the threat comes from temptation, and in the other it comes from boredom, but the problem is the same: controlling the competing emotion is necessary in order to keep it from leading to behaviors that will be pleasant in the short term but harmful in the long term.

Inhibiting destructive responses to provocation

A further benefit of emotional regulation is that it allows you to inhibit your immediate destructive response to provocation from others. One of the factors that most strongly influences the development of interpersonal conflict is the response you make after you have been provoked by another person. Unfortunately, the number and variety of such provocations are extensive—we never seem to experience any shortage of insults, slights, broken promises, missed appointments, thoughtless comments, inconsiderate behavior, sarcasm, hostile teasing and so on. When faced with such misbehavior by others, our immediate and uncensored response is often to retaliate in kind: to match insult with insult, sarcasm with sarcasm. ("Not only does my mother *not* resemble a badger; the reptilian characteristics of your family would be amusing if they weren't so frightening.") The result of responding in this way is sadly predictable. Retaliatory responses often lead to further escalation of a conflict, and can easily produce an escalatory spiral in which an initially minor disagreement can mutate into a much more serious one.

Of course, there *is* another way to respond to provocation. Instead of acting on the immediate and impulsive desire to retaliate, it is also possible to inhibit that response and substitute it with a more constructive one. That is, rather than responding to an insult with an insult, you might say nothing, use humor to change the mood or try to figure out what prompted the provocation in the first place. The good news is that responding in this way avoids further inflaming the situation, and thus increases the likelihood that a full-scale conflict can be avoided. The bad news is that this kind of responding is hard to do! Our initial emotional responses can be very powerful; what makes measured, constructive responding possible at all is the ability to regulate the immediate, impulsive, "hot" emotional response often triggered by the initial provocation.

Acting correctly despite pressure to do otherwise

There are other benefits in emotional regulation, but let me mention just one more—a benefit that may be somewhat less obvious than the ones presented thus far: good emotional regulation makes it easier for us to act in ways that are correct but might be unpopular with others. One of the most significant barriers to acting in accordance with our personal standards and ideals is that sometimes this behavior conflicts with the wishes of others. When that happens, we may experience considerable disapproval, and few things are more unpleasant to members of our species than social disapproval. A teenager who feels pressured to smoke and drink by peers, for example, is attempting to live up to a personal standard of behavior, but is faced with social pressure to do otherwise. Without an ability to regulate the negative emotion caused by social disapproval, fear of such disapproval is often powerful enough to override your best efforts to do the right thing.

How do you regulate your emotions?

The advantages of successfully regulating your own emotions are clear and compelling; luckily, you also have a variety of techniques available to aid in such regulation. Although it is a bit of an oversimplification, I think it is possible to identify five broad methods that are frequently used. Each technique can be effective if used in the right way at the right time, but some may be more generally useful than others.

1. Using inhibition
One fairly straightforward technique is inhibition. Using this method involves suppressing or stifling unpleasant

emotions when they occur, controlling or completely eliminating outward signs of emotions and in general "clamping down" on unwanted emotions through deliberate and conscious effort. This technique can be especially useful when you find yourself in situations where the display of an emotion is inappropriate; it is, for example, usually considered good form to suppress one's laughter at a funeral. However, there may also be some costs to using inhibition. Research suggests that this technique requires more effort than some other techniques. One result of this is that we may suffer more cognitive impairment to our attention and memory when employing this method; another result is that inhibition can produce a higher level of stressful physiological arousal.

2. Using cognitive reappraisal

A second regulation technique is cognitive reappraisal. This is a general technique that can encompass several specific methods, but what they all have in common is that in some way you try to mentally change the situation to produce a more desirable emotional state. For example, someone who is about to take an important examination may tell herself that it is "only a test," that it only measures knowledge in one narrow area and that it is *not* a broad measure of her overall worth. By controlling the way that she defines the situation, she reduces the level of anxiety that she is feeling. Similarly, a man who does not receive a highly anticipated promotion may tell himself that the method used for making the promotion decision was flawed and did not recognize his clear strengths, so it is not a good indicator of his value to the organization.

In essence, cognitive reappraisal allows you to change the personal meaning that you attach to a situation, and thus change the emotional consequences of success or failure. This technique can be effectively used both before some emotion-producing event (as in the "examination" example above) or afterward, as when the employee cognitively reappraises the promotion decision after the fact. Interestingly, research that has directly compared suppression and cognitive reappraisal has consistently found that reappraisal produces the same benefits as suppression (and in some cases, greater benefits) without the negative consequences that suppression can produce.

3. Shifting attention
In this method you handle negative emotions by turning attention away from the distress-producing stimulus and toward something less arousing. For example, someone who responds to high levels of anxiety at home by focusing his attention increasingly on his job is employing a form of this technique. Similarly, someone in the dentist's chair might use this technique—they may, for instance, call up vivid memories of their recent vacation on a beautiful Caribbean beach in order to distract themselves from the high-pitched whine of the drill and

the alarmingly impressive array of sharp instruments gleaming on the dentist's tray.

4. Using active planning

In this technique, you control your emotional reactions by formulating specific plans for dealing with the causes of those emotions. For instance, someone who is highly anxious because of his serious financial difficulties might respond by developing a comprehensive plan to reduce unnecessary expenses, stopping running up credit card debt, implementing a strict weekly budget and so on.

As you may imagine, active planning is in general a very good strategy, and often leads not only to short-term emotional regulation but also to better long-term solutions. The biggest shortcoming of this method is probably that it is not appropriate in all settings; sometimes the situation requiring emotional regulation (for example, rushing your injured child to a hospital accident and emergency department) does not allow for the development of long-term planning of solutions. (First I'll have the car tuned up, check the gas, prepare some snacks for the hospital ...)

5. Enlisting aid

This final method is in a way similar to active planning. In this technique, you respond to the need for emotional regulation by seeking help from others. The help can take the form of practical, concrete aid such as money, goods or effort. Alternatively, it may consist of emotional support rather than anything material. This method resembles active planning in that both techniques involve you trying to *solve* the problem that is causing the distress, rather than simply suppressing emotions, cognitively reappraising the situation or distracting yourself from the stressor.

Regulating emotions in other people

Although regulating your own emotions could never be described as a simple task, in most cases it *is* probably easier than regulating the emotions of other people. When attempting to control your own moods and feelings, you have the advantage of direct control over your behavior. That is, it may be difficult sometimes to forgo the cinnamon bun, or to exercise as regularly as you should, but at least the behavior you are trying to influence is your own. Attempting to regulate emotions in other people is more difficult because you have no direct control over them; instead, you must try to influence them indirectly through your words and deeds. How do you accomplish this?

One common occasion when you attempt to regulate the emotions of others occurs when you *soothe or comfort* other people. Everyone has had the experience of trying to help a friend or loved one who is suffering from high levels of stress, fear or anxiety. Similarly, we have all had the experience of trying to calm someone down who was in an angry state. Negative emotional states such as this are distressing to those who are experiencing them, and often to us as well; therefore skill in calming down people who are experiencing high levels of these emotions can be extremely useful.

Similarly, you sometimes find it necessary to cheer up or encourage people who are sad or depressed. In this case the goal is not to calm them down—depressed people tend to be pretty calm already. In this situation the goal is in a sense the opposite—to move the mood, spirit and energy level up rather than down. Because mood regulation is still the goal, however, some of the same techniques used in soothing may still be appropriate. The use of humor, for example, may potentially be helpful for calming an angry person, cheering up a sad person or soothing a stressed one. Offering words of sympathy and emotional support can also be useful for either soothing a fearful friend or encouraging a depressed one.

A third form of emotional regulation is somewhat different from the first two—it involves creating motivation or enthusiasm in another person or group. The goal in this case is not so much to reduce negative emotions or increase positive ones, but to increase others' eagerness to work hard and tackle a challenge. This skill can be especially useful when others have been frustrated by repeated failures or setbacks. This form of emotional regulation is, then, somewhat more goal-focused than the previous two forms.

TESTS

This chapter concludes with a set of six tests to measure skill in the area of emotional regulation:

- Three tests to measure the ability to regulate your own emotions (self-report, multirater and performance tests).
- Three tests to measure the ability to regulate the emotions of others (self-report, multirater and performance tests).

TEST 13

Regulating your own emotions
Self-report test

Indicate how well each of the following statements describes you. Be as frank and honest as possible in your answers; this test can only be useful if your answers are accurate. In responding to each item, use one of the following choices:

1 = This is **never** true of me
2 = This is **rarely** true of me
3 = This is **sometimes** true of me
4 = This is **frequently** true of me
5 = This is **always** true of me

☐ 1. When I begin to feel powerful emotions, I am good at controlling them.

☐ 2. I let my emotions get the better of me.

☐ 3. I find that my moods are strong enough to control my behavior.

☐ 4. I get so angry that I cannot control myself.

☐ 5. I can stay on an even emotional keel.

☐ 6. It is easy for everyone to tell when I am unhappy.

☐ 7. I am the master of my feelings.

☐ 8. My moods are uncontrollable.

☐ 9. I keep a tight grip on my emotions.

☐ 10. I can make my good moods last a long time.

TEST 14

Regulating your own emotions
Multirater test

At least one person who knows you well should complete this test, answering the questions about you. It is even better if several people complete the test, so that you can get a broader picture of how others view your EQ abilities. Once they have done so, you can score the tests using the instructions provided (see page 171).

Indicate how well each of the following statements describes the person you are being asked to rate. Be as frank and honest as possible in your answers; this test can only be useful if your answers are accurate. In responding to each item, use one of the following choices:

1 = This is **never** true of the person
2 = This is **rarely** true of the person
3 = This is **sometimes** true of the person
4 = This is **frequently** true of the person
5 = This is **always** true of the person

☐ 1. This person is good at regulating their emotions.

☐ 2. This person does not "fly off the handle" when angry.

☐ 3. This person's emotions are obvious for all to see.

☐ 4. This person is not overwhelmed by their emotions.

☐ 5. This person is able to control their feelings without others ever realizing it.

☐ 6. This person is skilled at mastering their emotional responses to events.

☐ 7. This person is unable to successfully control their moods.

☐ 8. This person wears their emotions "on their sleeve."

☐ 9. When this person is disappointed, it is clear to everyone.

☐ 10. This person seems at the mercy of their emotions.

TEST 15

Regulating your own emotions
Performance test

Each of the following questions describes a situation in which you might find yourself, and in which you are experiencing an emotion. After each description you are asked to indicate the *most effective* way—or ways—to regulate that emotion. In some cases only one response is likely to be effective; in others there will be more than one. Circle all the ways that you think would be *likely*—not just theoretically possible—to be effective in that situation.

1. You are feeling a great deal of tension because an important deadline is coming up at work. Which of the following would be an effective way to reduce your tension?

   a. Exercising
   b. Working longer hours
   c. Meditating
   d. Distracting yourself with a pleasant activity

2. You are feeling angry at a member of your family because of something he said to you. Which of the following would be an effective way to reduce your anger?

a. Yelling at the person to release your anger
b. Asking the person for an apology
c. Imagining why the person might have said it
d. Making a list of the person's good qualities

3. You have been feeling sad for a few days. Which of the following would be an effective way to reduce your sadness?

   a. Spending some time alone to reflect
   b. Going out with friends to a party
   c. Having a drink or two
   d. Talking to your best friend about it

4. You wake up one day in a wonderful mood. Which of the following would be an effective way to prolong this mood?

   a. Going to work early
   b. Doing something nice for someone else
   c. Taking a long lunch
   d. Asking the boss for a pay increase

5. You are feeling ashamed because you forgot your spouse's birthday. Which of the following would be an effective way to reduce these feelings?

a. Thinking about something else
b. Not telling anyone else about your oversight
c. Apologizing to your spouse
d. Telling yourself that you will buy your spouse a wonderful gift next year

6. You are feeling somewhat envious of a friend because she recently got a big promotion at work and you did not. Which of the following would be an effective way to reduce your envy?

a. Gossiping about your friend
b. Reminding yourself of all the good things you have
c. Concealing this feeling
d. Congratulating your friend

7. Your child is throwing one tantrum after another and you are becoming very frustrated. Which of the following would be an effective way to reduce your frustration?

a. Counting slowly to 10
b. Venting your frustration by shouting at the child

c. Telling the child to be quiet

d. Imagining a cool and peaceful scene

8. You have been involved in a conflict with someone at work for several days, and are feeling nervous and unhappy as a result. Which of the following would be an effective way to reduce these feelings?

   a. Reaching out to the other person and trying to find a solution to the conflict

   b. Giving in to the other person to end the conflict

   c. Standing firm and waiting for the other person to concede

   d. Deciding that the issue is not worth the anxiety, and compromising with the other person

9. You and your best friend have had a disagreement, and the relationship is somewhat strained at the moment; you feel cross and unhappy as a result. Which of the following would be an effective way to reduce these feelings?

   a. Avoiding your best friend

b. Complaining about the friend to your spouse

c. Trying to understand your friend's perspective

d. Telling your friend what you are feeling

10. An important project deadline is approaching in your job, and you are experiencing considerable stress as the amount of work remaining becomes clear. Which of the following would be an effective way to reduce these feelings?

a. Trying to avoid thinking about the deadline

b. Developing a step-by-step plan to complete the work on time

c. Enlisting the aid of others in the organization

d. Waiting until the last minute and then working around the clock to get the job done

TEST 16

Regulating others' emotions
Self-report test

Indicate how well each of the following statements describes you. Be as frank and honest as possible in your answers; this test can only be useful if your answers are accurate. In responding to each item, use one of the following choices:

1 = This is **never** true of me
2 = This is **rarely** true of me
3 = This is **sometimes** true of me
4 = This is **frequently** true of me
5 = This is **always** true of me

1. When other people are angry, I am good at calming them down.

2. When my spouse is feeling depressed, I can cheer them up.

3. I am not successful at soothing my friends when they are stressed.

4. When coworkers get frustrated, I know how to encourage them and restore their motivation.

☐ 5. When someone is feeling bad, I'm not much good at cheering them up.

☐ 6. I'm able to use humor effectively to defuse emotional situations.

☐ 7. When I try to calm down an angry person, it makes things worse.

☐ 8. I don't know what to say to someone who is depressed.

☐ 9. I find it difficult to motivate other people.

☐ 10. When two of my friends are having an argument, I am good at smoothing things over.

TEST 17

Regulating others' emotions
Multirater test

At least one person who knows you well should complete this test, answering the questions about you. It is even better if several people complete the test, so that you can get a broader picture of how others view your EQ abilities. Once they have done so, you can score the tests using the instructions provided (see page 171).

Indicate how well each of the following statements describes the person you are being asked to rate. Be as frank and honest as possible in your answers; this test can only be useful if your answers are accurate. In responding to each item, use one of the following choices:

1 = This is **never** true of the person
2 = This is **rarely** true of the person
3 = This is **sometimes** true of the person
4 = This is **frequently** true of the person
5 = This is **always** true of the person

☐ 1. This person can calm and reassure others in times of stress.

☐ 2. This person is not skilled at cheering up someone who is unhappy.

☐ 3. This person can reason with someone who is angry.

☐ 4. When others are frustrated, this person is good at getting them back on track.

☐ 5. This person's attempts to be a calming influence actually make things worse.

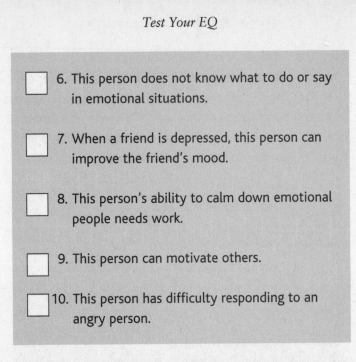

6. This person does not know what to do or say in emotional situations.

7. When a friend is depressed, this person can improve the friend's mood.

8. This person's ability to calm down emotional people needs work.

9. This person can motivate others.

10. This person has difficulty responding to an angry person.

TEST 18

Regulating others' emotions
Performance test

Each of the following questions describes a situation involving another person, in which that person is experiencing an emotion. After each description you are asked to indicate the *most effective* way, or ways, in which you could regulate that emotion. In some cases only one response is likely to be effective; in others there will be more than one. Circle all the ways that you think would be *likely*—not just theoretically possible—to be effective in that situation.

1. A friend has come to you very upset over some personal problem she is having. Which of the following is an effective method of helping to reduce her level of distress?

   a. Offering her your advice about how to solve the problem
   b. Listening without emotion
   c. Listening and encouraging her to keep talking
   d. Telling her everything will be all right

2. A coworker has been sad and depressed for several days. Which of the following is an effective method of helping improve his mood?

   a. Asking him why he is feeling sad
   b. Telling him to snap out of it
   c. Getting him to join you in an activity you know he likes
   d. Telling him about a time when you were depressed

3. You and your fellow employees have been working very hard lately, and you would like to improve the general emotional climate on

the job. Which of the following is an effective method of helping to achieve this?

a. Making some cookies and cakes and taking them to work
b. Asking your fellow employees to cheer up
c. Learning a new joke to tell them
d. Making sarcastic comments about the boss

4. Your spouse is angry with you because you forgot to do an important errand you had promised to do. Which of the following is an effective method of reducing your spouse's anger?

a. Avoiding your spouse until things calm down
b. Reminding your spouse about times when they forgot things
c. Apologizing to your spouse
d. Promising not to make this mistake in the future

5. You have an assistant who has skills and ability, but is not very motivated. Which of the following is an effective method of improving the assistant's motivation?

    a. Praising the assistant for their skills

    b. Telling the assistant how much you value them

    c. Telling the assistant to improve or be fired

    d. Suggesting to the assistant that they come to work earlier

6. Your boss has become very demanding as a project deadline approaches, and a coworker comes to you highly stressed and upset. Which of the following is an effective method of reducing the coworker's distress?

    a. Letting him vent his feelings to you

    b. Indicating that you understand exactly how he feels

    c. Telling him to work harder

    d. Making rude jokes about the boss

7. Your son is ill, and becomes very disappointed about not being able to attend his best friend's birthday party. Which of the following is an effective method of helping him feel better?

    a. Telling him that life is often unfair

    b. Telling him this is too small a matter to be upset about

    c. Saying how sorry you are that this has happened

    d. Saying that the party was probably not much fun anyway

8. Your spouse is very nervous about giving an important presentation at work. Which of the following is an effective method of reducing your spouse's level of distress?

    a. Telling your spouse not to worry

    b. Offering to let your spouse practice the talk on you

    c. Taking your spouse to see a film as a distraction

    d. Giving your spouse a relaxing massage

9. Your boss is a blustery man who often uses an angry tone when talking to employees. Which of the following is an effective method of responding to the boss?

    a. Answering calmly in response

    b. Avoiding the boss whenever possible

    c. Using humor when appropriate

d. Responding with an angry tone of your own

10. Your coworker is often in a cynical and negative mood, dissatisfied with almost everything. Which of the following is an effective method of responding to him when he acts this way?

   a. Using humor to improve the mood
   b. Not responding
   c. Agreeing with him
   d. Telling him he is wrong

5

USING EMOTIONS
EFFECTIVELY

WE COME NOW to the final skill contributing to emotional intelligence: the ability to use emotions in order to be more effective in life. In a way, this skill resembles the emotional regulation skill described in the previous chapter (see page 78); using emotions, like regulating them, is a more active form of EQ than simply recognizing and understanding emotional states. In addition, the *use* of emotions can be seen as growing naturally out of regulating them—in fact, regulation is really a kind of use. The dividing line between these final two skills is therefore a little fuzzy at times. Ultimately, of course, all four skills are deeply inter-twined in everyday life: we need to recognize emotions in order to understand how they will operate in any given situation; we need to know how they work in order to effectively use them; and we need to regulate them appropriately so that our attempts to use them will be successful.

What, exactly, is meant when we say that people can successfully "use" their emotions? Perhaps the most useful way to answer this question is to think of emotions as a kind of natural resource. In order to achieve certain goals, this resource can be very helpful; for other goals it might be much less useful. Using emotions successfully means being able—when appropriate—to harness the power of this resource in order to reach a goal. There are several ways in which this might happen.

Using emotions to enhance your performance

One way in which emotions can be used is to enhance your performance in some fashion. For example, emotions can be employed to improve your ability to persist in the pursuit of some goal. Imagine, for example, an overweight young man who is on a diet. As we have noted in previous chapters, dieting is a difficult thing to do, especially when, as always happens, the food allowed by the diet becomes less alluring, and temptations arise with greater and greater frequency. What can be done?

In this case, the young man may try to recruit some powerful emotions to help him remain faithful to the diet. He may, for example, select some photographs that depict him at his heaviest and least attractive. He may then place these photographs on the refrigerator, on cupboard and pantry doors, and in any other location that he might approach when his resolve weakens and he begins to look for foods more satisfying than celery and rice cakes. The sight of the photographs portraying him in the worst light will help re-create the emotional state that led him to adopt the diet in the first place. In this case, therefore, successfully using emotions would consist of harnessing the motivating power of shame, embarrassment and social anxiety.

To take another example, imagine a young woman who has aspirations to become a writer. Writing can be a lonely business, requiring you to work steadily for long periods of time without social contact, encouragement or positive feedback; it is not uncommon to find that people eventually give up rather than continue under such circumstances. (At a conference I once attended, the psychologist Robert Arkin offered what he called "Arkin's First Law: when given a choice between writing and any other activity, people will always choose the other activity.") In the case of our hypothetical young woman, how could she maintain her motivation?

One solution could be to cover the wall of her work space with the rejection letters she has received from magazine editors and book publishers. Each time she sees them, she becomes angry, and it fuels her determination to keep working and prove the critics wrong. In this case, she has harnessed the power of anger and resentment to advance her goal. Of course, if the effect of seeing these rejections is not to make her angry, but simply to depress her, then this is not an effective strategy. The person skilled in the use of emotions will recognize this and change strategies. (The unskilled person will, presumably, slowly go mad!)

To give one more example, a technique that people sometimes use to great effect as they attempt to persist in a difficult course of action is to arrange things so that a failure to persist will lead to a highly undesirable outcome. A man trying to quit smoking may write out a large check to an organization whose goals and politics he absolutely detests—and then give the check to a trusted friend with strict instructions to send it to the organization in question if he should ever start smoking again. In this case, the man is recruiting the anguish and revulsion he would feel if his check were delivered to bolster his efforts to avoid cigarettes.

In addition to using emotions to enhance our persistence over the long term, we can also use them to enhance our performance in more immediate situations. The purest version of this strategy can be seen among actors, songwriters, novelists and other artists. In order to play a character in the throes of emotional turmoil, actors look for life experiences they can draw upon to portray such turmoil more effectively. To create powerful songs of heartache, songwriters mine their personal unhappiness. Novelists employ imagination to transform their own emotional experiences into compelling narratives. In less dramatic ways, however, we all engage in the same kind of activities every day, as we try to use our emotions and our emotional history to help us accomplish our objectives.

For example, imagine an executive who is about to make an important presentation to senior management. The presentation has been carefully prepared and rehearsed; the handouts and ancillary materials are ready; all physical preparations have been made. There is no reason why the presentation should not go well . . . except for the presenter. For some reason he finds himself in a rather "blah" mood that day, with low energy and weak enthusiasm. In such a situation, he might try to find ways to harness emotion to prepare for the presentation. He may find that giving himself a pep talk would be helpful. He could make use of motivational tapes that exhort the listener to strive for excellence and reach for the stars. A common and often helpful technique that he might employ is to use music to induce a desired emotional state. In this case, listening to something loud, or stirring, or angry could do the trick—whatever it takes to help create in him a sense of energy and enthusiasm during his presentation.

Using emotions to enhance your general well-being

A somewhat different way in which emotions may be used has less to do with improving performance per se, and more to do with the generally beneficial effects of positive emotions. It has been argued by some psychologists that one effect of positive emotions is that they at least temporarily broaden the range of thoughts and actions available to you—that is, positive emotions tend to make you more open to experience, more likely to explore, to be creative and to try new things. In contrast, negative emotions generally tend to have the reverse effect; they narrow your focus and constrict the ways in which you engage with the world. When you are fearful or angry, for example, you become less likely to explore, reach out or be creative; instead you tend to withdraw, focus on the problem and "hunker down" emotionally.

According to this view, the long-term effect of being open to new experience is that it helps build your personal resources by making you more receptive to meeting new people, going to new places and learning new things. The more open you are to new experiences, the larger your network of social support becomes, and the better able you are to cope with stressful or upsetting events in your life.

The long-term effect of being relatively closed to new experience is to prevent this kind of expansion of your social resources, eventually making you less able to weather the stresses and strains of life. The emotionally intelligent use of emotions, then, should include an ability to create or maintain positive emotional states so as to enlarge your personal resources as much as possible. In particular, skill in this area should allow you to:

1. Prolong good moods when they occur.
2. Generate positive emotions even in the face of stresses that would ordinarily serve to destroy positive emotion and produce only negative mood states.

How can you do this? One frequently effective technique involves using humor. Research suggests that emotionally resilient people (that is, those who bounce back most effectively from stressful events) are in fact more likely to use humor as a coping mechanism. Responding to stresses in this way has several possible advantages over other coping strategies.

- Laughter can directly reduce the level of stress that you experience, providing an immediate benefit.
- Seeing the humorous side of stressful events helps you maintain a healthy perspective by reminding you that few problems are ever as big or as serious as your imagination can make them out to be. ("The nice thing about going bald is the money I save on combs.")
- When humor is used effectively, it not only benefits the person employing it but also provides enjoyment to others; in addition to its other benefits, then, the use of humor can also produce increased popularity. (This only applies, however, to the *effective* use of humor—the frequent telling of bad jokes is not a recommended method for achieving popularity!)

Another technique that can help maintain positive moods in the face of stress involves using effective emotional regulation strategies. That is, some of the techniques outlined in the previous chapter as effective ways to *control* emotions may also be useful here. In particular, the techniques of cognitive reappraisal (see page 79) and active planning (see page 81) can be very useful for creating and maintaining positive moods. For example, appraisal strategies that help minimize the importance of negative outcomes, or emphasize their transitory nature, tend to improve the emotional resilience of those who employ them. ("Failing that exam was due to some bad luck, and I'll do better next time.")

Using emotions to influence others

Emotions can also be used to influence other people. Life is filled with situations in which it is to our advantage to persuade others to adopt our opinion or attitude. We persuade others to spend their lives with us, to have children with us, to change jobs for us, and to pick up and move to a new city or country with us. We persuade clients to buy our products, employees to work harder and bosses to give us pay increases. Inducing others to act in the ways we desire can in a sense be considered the primary goal in a social species such as ours, and it would seem that a well-developed emotional intelligence must include this. As has often been the case, there are lots of ways in which emotions could be used for this purpose, but let us focus on four.

Intimidation

Intimidation relies on the ability to create fear in others; the intended result is to be seen as a powerful figure and to gain the others' compliance. In the right circumstances, this can be an effective technique, but there are also costs.

One obvious cost is that frequent use of intimidation tends to rather substantially decrease your popularity. Another potential problem is that the threat made by the would-be intimidator must be credible; otherwise the threat is seen as empty and the intimidator is viewed as ridiculous. My three-year-old niece once gazed up at her grandmother, and in an attempt to get her to play, solemnly said, "If you don't, you will never see me again." This was not, as you might imagine, a threat that struck much terror into her grandmother's heart. Such toothless threats, when made by adults rather than toddlers, are seen as considerably less cute and endearing.

Supplication

Another influence technique is supplication—defined as inducing feelings of sympathy and compassion in others, with the goal of receiving assistance from them. Examples of this technique would be a worker who asks for help from others because he lacks the expertise to do the job himself, or the wife who professes ignorance about anything to do with cars when requesting her husband's help with her malfunctioning vehicle. Like intimidation, supplication can be a useful strategy in the right circumstances, but it also has limits and drawbacks. The biggest problem may be that using it too frequently creates an unfavorable image in others' minds—of an incompetent person unable to meet responsibilities, or of a perpetual complainer unwilling to do so.

Flattery
When you employ this technique, you praise other people with the goal of making them like you; the emotions you are trying to create are gratitude and affection. The student who compliments his teacher before an examination ("My, that is an attractive feather boa you are wearing today, Mrs. Jones!"), or the employee who starts each day by praising his boss ("My, that is an attractive feather boa you are wearing today, Mr. Williams!"), are both using this strategy.

Flattery has been around for virtually as long as people have been able to form words with which to flatter, and its benefits are well known. Unfortunately, so are its drawbacks. Flattery that is too frequent, too effusive or too extravagant will not have the desired effect but will instead result in the flatterer being branded with unpleasant labels that are better left unstated. The emotionally intelligent person, on the other hand, is able to use flattery in the right way—sparingly and plausibly—so as to gain its benefits without incurring its costs.

Guilt

The fourth technique involves inducing the emotion of guilt in others, with the intention of producing a feeling of obligation that will lead them to do something you want them to do. The mother who tells her grown children that it's all right if they don't come home for Christmas (pause), that it's not a big deal (sigh), that she will *probably* still be alive next year (cough)—that is someone who is using guilt like a master!

The key drawback of using this technique is that repeated use can create resentment toward the guilt inducer, which may reduce the technique's effectiveness. In addition, unlike some of the other techniques, guilt is probably effective for only a small number of targets—it is difficult, for instance, to make anyone *other* than your immediate family feel guilty over not being with you during the holidays.

It may sound from this discussion that using emotions to influence others is somehow underhand and distasteful—threats, flattery, begging and guilt don't seem all that noble. While it is certainly possible to think of instances in which these techniques are used crudely and nakedly, used in moderation, and in appropriate ways, there is nothing inherently wrong with the use of any of them. Letting others see how angry you will be can be seen as a threat, *or* as providing them with valuable information about how important an issue is to you. Flattering someone by telling them an outright lie is hard to defend, but offering compliments that genuinely reflect your feelings about someone do not seem so bad, even if they *do* make that person like you more!

Using emotions to handle conflict better

A final occasion in which emotions can be used effectively presents itself when interpersonal conflicts arise. Disagreements with others are inevitable, of course, but the *way* in which they unfold is to a considerable degree under your control. In particular, the extent to which harmful and hurtful emotions become part of social conflict is something that the emotionally intelligent person can successfully influence.

The most important way to influence the course of a conflict is to respond appropriately at the very beginning—when you are first provoked by another. Destructive responses at this stage tend to make conflicts worse, while constructive responses tend to make things better. One potentially destructive way in which you can respond to provocation is by *not* expressing your emotional reactions. Instead you conceal these emotions from others and keep them inside. While there is some value in not expressing all of your emotional responses, hiding relevant feelings can interfere with healthy relationships. Hidden emotions can also negatively affect job performance, physical health and psychological well-being.

There is a variety of reasons why you might keep your feelings hidden—belief that they can't be expressed properly, fear of making the situation worse, or fear of losing acceptance or validation from others. However, when unexpressed emotions are interfering with relationships or job performance, then it is necessary to address them. Providing information to others about how you feel and why can be useful to them; it tells them the issue is important to you and that it is something which should not be overlooked or taken lightly. It also indicates that you care about your relationships with others. The goal here is to express your emotions appropriately and in a way that casts no blame.

A second destructive way in which you can respond to provocation is by expressing your emotions in a way that makes the conflict worse. Clearly displaying your anger through raising your voice or pounding the table may feel good, but it typically makes the other person feel attacked—and produces similar responses in return. Using sarcasm and ridicule (even when it seems to be richly deserved!) also tends to "personalize" the disagreement and make the other party even more hostile than they were before. The careless expression of these "toxic" emotions often leads to an escalating cycle of hostility and resentment.

What is the solution? As you might guess, it lies in

finding ways to respond to provocation that inhibit the expression of destructive emotions, and instead invite the other party to participate in a joint effort to resolve the issue in question. Therefore one part of emotionally intelligent responding to conflict is to *not* immediately respond to provocation. This approach helps to prevent you from responding in hasty and ill-advised ways. Delaying your response, and letting things calm down before reacting, is an important first step to managing emotions during conflict.

The next step is to enlist the cooperation of the other party, and some of the techniques already discussed can be helpful. For example, taking the perspective of the other person (see page 40) is a good way to understand the reasoning behind their position. Another good technique is to make overtures to the other party to work together to find solutions. Asking the other party questions designed to learn their vital interests, and brainstorming with them to generate solutions, are excellent ways to defuse the negative emotions that conflict often creates and instead create an environment in which the two parties involved in the conflict work "side by side" instead of going "head to head."

TESTS

This chapter concludes with five tests to measure skill in the area of using emotions effectively:

- Two tests to measure the ability to use your own emotions (self-report and performance tests).
- Three tests to measure the ability to use the emotions of others (self-report, multirater and performance tests).

TEST 19

Using your own emotions
Self-report test

Indicate how well each of the following statements describes you. Be as frank and honest as possible in your answers; this test can only be useful if your answers are accurate. In responding to each item, use one of the following choices:

1 = This is **never** true of me
2 = This is **rarely** true of me
3 = This is **sometimes** true of me
4 = This is **frequently** true of me
5 = This is **always** true of me

[ ] 1. When necessary, I can make myself feel enthusiastic.

[ ] 2. I lose motivation when I'm working toward a long-term goal.

☐ 3. I can keep myself in a good mood even when things aren't going perfectly.

☐ 4. It's more likely that my emotions will control me than it is that I will control my emotions.

☐ 5. When I fail, I use my disappointment to motivate me to try harder.

☐ 6. It's hard for me to put myself into a particular mood.

☐ 7. If I act cheerful and happy, I start to really feel that way.

☐ 8. When I am in a bad mood, it is difficult to make myself feel happy.

☐ 9. If the situation calls for it, I can put myself in an energetic and upbeat mood.

☐ 10. I have difficulty maintaining a good mood for very long.

TEST 20

Using your own emotions
Performance test

Each of the following questions describes a situation in which you might find it helpful to use your emotions in some way. After each description you will be asked to indicate the *most effective* way—or ways—in which you could use that emotion. In some cases only one response is likely to be effective; in others there will be more than one. Circle all the ways that you think would be *likely*—not just theoretically possible—to be effective in that situation.

1. Although you don't feel especially upbeat today, you know that it will be crucial for you to appear enthusiastic at an important meeting at work. Which of the following would be an effective method of creating this emotion?

   a. Quiet meditation before the meeting
   b. Vigorous exercise before the meeting
   c. Watching an exciting video before the meeting
   d. Listening to lively, upbeat music before the meeting

2. You stopped smoking two months ago. However, recently you have begun to feel your motivation slip, and you are worried that you will start smoking again. Which of the following would be an effective method of resisting this temptation?

   a. Having one or two cigarettes to kill the temptation
   b. Telling yourself repeatedly, "Don't think about cigarettes!"
   c. Visiting some antismoking Web sites and looking at pictures of diseased lungs
   d. Making a list of the reasons why you quit and seeing if you still agree with them

3. You are trying to impress upon your subordinates the importance of showing up for work on time, and you are having difficulty getting the message across. Which of the following would be an effective method of accomplishing this goal?

   a. Reading them the relevant sections from the company regulations
   b. Asking sarcastically if the job is interfering with their sleeping habits

    c. Asking them to try harder as a favor to
       you

    d. Threatening them

4. You are in a play being put on by your local
   theater, and your role requires you to deliver
   a sad and moving speech. Which of the
   following would be an effective method of
   helping you portray your role?

    a. To maintain "freshness," only learning
       your lines well enough to paraphrase them

    b. Before performing, recalling a time of
       sadness in your life

    c. Making your mind a blank before taking
       the stage

    d. Pinching yourself hard before delivering
       your speech

5. Everything that could go wrong this week did
   go wrong—both at work and at home. Which
   of the following would be an effective
   method of keeping your mood from
   becoming too depressed?

    a. Engaging in some strenuous physical
       exercise

b. Trying to look for the funny side of the things
c. Trying to suppress your feelings of sadness
d. Treating yourself to a favorite activity or meal

6. You are working on a long-term home redecorating project, and are trying to keep your motivation up for the duration of the job. Which of the following would be effective for maintaining your motivation?

a. Giving yourself a small reward as you finish each part of the job
b. Giving yourself a pep talk every few days
c. Looking frequently at a picture of what the finished project will look like
d. Not thinking about how tedious the work has become

7. You are somewhat envious of a colleague at work who seems to be progressing faster than you. Which of the following would be an effective method of dealing with these feelings?

a. Letting your envy spur you to work harder

b. Stopping comparing yourself to him and just accepting yourself
c. Trying to sabotage him
d. Talking to him honestly about your feelings

8. Things have been going quite well recently and you are in a very good mood. Which of the following would be an effective method of prolonging this mood as long as possible?

a. Tackling some new and difficult challenge in your life
b. Doing something generous for another person
c. Avoiding any changes in your routine
d. Using the opportunity to do the tasks that you hate the most

9. You have never been very close to your older brother because of the way he treated you when you were growing up. Now, however, he is seriously ill and needs your help. Which of the following would be an effective way of dealing with your feelings toward him?

a. Recalling the times when he was cruel to you
b. Trying to suppress memories of his behavior in the past
c. Recalling the times when he was nice to you
d. Imagining how you would feel if you refused to help a family member

10. You have been working extra hours to earn enough money to buy your spouse an expensive gift, but the work is tedious. Which of the following would be an effective way of dealing with these feelings?

a. Daydreaming a lot to make the time go faster
b. Forgetting the expensive gift and stopping working the extra hours
c. Imagining how delighted your spouse will be with the gift
d. Keeping an eye on the clock and counting the hours

TEST 21

Using others' emotions
Self-report test

Indicate how well each of the following statements describes you. Be as frank and honest as possible in your answers; this test can only be useful if your answers are accurate. In responding to each item, use one of the following choices:

1 = This is **never** true of me
2 = This is **rarely** true of me
3 = This is **sometimes** true of me
4 = This is **frequently** true of me
5 = This is **always** true of me

☐ 1. If someone I am competing with becomes angry, I use that to my advantage.

☐ 2. I find it difficult to induce emotions in other people.

☐ 3. When someone is in a good mood, I don't take advantage of it to ask a favor.

☐ 4. I use mild threats to accomplish my goals.

☐ 5. I use guilt to influence another's behavior.

☐ 6. I do favors for other people with the hope that they will do something for me in return.

☐ 7. I am skilled at influencing others' emotions.

☐ 8. I find it difficult to influence other people when they are emotional.

☐ 9. I find it difficult to use others' strong emotions for my own benefit.

☐ 10. It is difficult for me to influence others' emotions.

TEST 22

Using others' emotions
Multirater test

At least one person who knows you well should complete this test, answering the questions about you. It is even better if several people complete the test, so that you can get a broader picture of how others view your EQ abilities. Once they have done so, you can score the tests using the instructions provided (see page 172).

Indicate how well each of the following statements

describes the person you are being asked to rate. Be as frank and honest as possible in your answers; this test can only be useful if your answers are accurate. In responding to each item, use one of the following choices:

1 = This is **never** true of the person
2 = This is **rarely** true of the person
3 = This is **sometimes** true of the person
4 = This is **frequently** true of the person
5 = This is **always** true of the person

1. This person is effective at using flattery to make others feel good.

2. This person successfully uses guilt to influence others.

3. This person is not effective at using others' emotions to accomplish their own goals.

4. This person has difficulty changing other people's moods.

5. If necessary, this person induces a little fear to get things done.

6. This person can take advantage of other people's emotional responses.

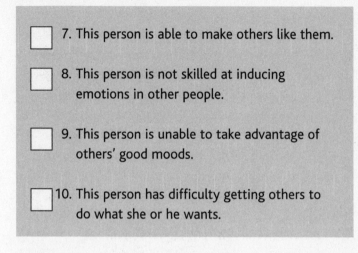

7. This person is able to make others like them.

8. This person is not skilled at inducing emotions in other people.

9. This person is unable to take advantage of others' good moods.

10. This person has difficulty getting others to do what she or he wants.

TEST 23

Using others' emotions
Performance test

Each of the following questions describes a situation involving you and another person, where you might find it helpful to use the other's emotions in some way. After each description you will be asked to indicate the *most effective* way—or ways—in which you could use that emotion. In some cases only one response is likely to be effective; in others there will be more than one. Circle all the ways that you think would be *likely*—not just theoretically possible— to be effective in that situation.

1. You are working on a project, and find that you need to ask for help from someone on another work team. Which of the following would be effective methods of obtaining this help?

   a. Demanding that he help for the good of the organization
   b. Suggesting ways that you can be helpful to him as well
   c. Getting the boss to make him help
   d. Complimenting him before asking the favor

2. Your spouse is not very enthusiastic about spending the holidays with your family. Which of the following would be effective methods of changing your spouse's mind?

   a. Mentioning that you have spent the last three holidays with your spouse's family
   b. Trying to make a holiday with your family sound like fun
   c. Refusing to take no for an answer
   d. Looking hurt and sad

3. You are in charge of a work group made up of representatives from different departments of your organization. Which of the following would be effective methods of making this group work well together?

   a. Emphasizing the authority granted you by the boss
   b. Emphasizing that the group need only cooperate for a relatively short time
   c. Praising all the participants for their genuine accomplishments
   d. Emphasizing the benefits to each of the departments that success will bring

4. You are trying to persuade a group of neighbors to oppose the destruction of a local building. Which of the following would be effective methods of obtaining their support?

   a. Emphasizing the architectural beauty of the threatened building
   b. Emphasizing the possibility that the building will be replaced with something that will lower property values

c. Appealing to a sense of neighborhood loyalty

d. Telling them it is the right thing to do

5. You are quite concerned about the man your daughter is dating; he is significantly older than she is, and does not seem to have a steady job. Which of the following would be effective methods of expressing your concern?

a. Forbidding her to see him any more

b. Begging her not to see him any more

c. Asking her sarcastically when he last paid for a meal

d. Emphasizing how it hurts you to see her make a bad choice

6. You are planning to ask your boss for a raise. Which of the following would be effective methods of getting her agreement?

a. Waiting until she is in a good mood before asking

b. Reminding her of the hard work and sacrifices you have made for the job

c. Pointing out the ways in which you are superior to your coworkers

d. Claiming that you have another job offer

7. You are trying to convince your elderly and ailing father that it is time for him to move into a retirement home. Which of the following would be effective methods of convincing him?

a. Assuring him that he won't miss his old home

b. Telling him how friendly the retirement home staff will be

c. Emphasizing how concerned you are for his safety and health

d. Emphasizing the increased time he can spend with his grandchildren

8. You are trying to get your department to increase productivity by making some changes in job responsibilities. Which of the following would be effective methods of generating support for the changes in your staff?

a. Explaining your reasons and personally asking each of them for their help

b. Emphasizing the benefits for everyone if the plan works

c. Emphasizing that the changes are mandatory

d. Punishing anyone who does not comply

9. You and your spouse have been discussing the possibility of selling your house; you are somewhat reluctant to do so. Which of the following would be effective methods of convincing your spouse not to sell?

a. Telling your spouse that you refuse to move

b. Emphasizing to your spouse the sentimental value the house has to you

c. Talking about how sad you will be to move

d. Changing the subject

10. You have the responsibility for recruiting a new member of your work team and you have identified a good candidate. He is bright and ambitious but is somewhat ambivalent about coming to your group. Which of the following would be effective methods of convincing him to do so?

a. Emphasizing the bad points of his current work group
b. Emphasizing how working with your team offers the chance for faster advancement
c. Asking him as a personal favor
d. Refusing to take no for an answer

IMPROVING YOUR EMOTIONAL INTELLIGENCE

BY NOW YOU should have a pretty good idea about your abilities in the four areas of emotional intelligence: recognizing, understanding, regulating and using emotions. You have taken the tests, scored your answers and looked for areas in which you scored consistently high or low across multiple tests. So what can you do if there is an area in which you did not score very high? This chapter will present some practical advice on how you might improve in each of the four EQ areas; the resources section (see page 175) provides additional information that may also be of assistance.

As you know from reading this book, being an emotionally intelligent person is really a dynamic process. It requires give and take, learning and understanding, listening and communicating, thought and action. It requires recognizing how emotions, words and deeds (both yours and those of others) affect what's happening, or what's not happening. Being emotionally intelligent involves getting your needs met while at the same time meeting the needs of other people.

Before learning ways to improve your emotional intelligence, read the following two initial lessons. They represent themes that have been repeated throughout this book and are a good starting point for changing how you view emotions.

Emotional Lesson 1

To a considerable degree, emotions and how you respond to them are learned

Although certain emotions and facial expressions appear to be universal across all cultures, your *responses* to the emotions you feel, and the behaviors you enact, are learned. You've learned them through years of personal experience. You've been taught by your parents, siblings, teachers, friends and mentors. You've been influenced by your society's books, films, television, political leaders, sports heroes and other role models. Through all this, you've learned beneficial as well as ineffective and harmful ways of responding emotionally. Much of this learning occurred without any deliberate effort on your part. The essence of this lesson is that you have the ability to seek out and acquire *new* constructive responses as well.

Emotional Lesson 2

You control how you feel and respond

Although emotional situations can be powerful, to a greater degree than you may realize, you control your emotions; they don't control you. You control your behavior; it doesn't control you. If, say, you express your anger by ranting and raving, that's your choice. If you hold your anger inside, that's your choice too. You can affect the direction and intensity of your emotions. You have control. You have choices. You can change.

While it is the case that you can't always change what you want to change about *others*, you can change almost everything about yourself: how you perceive others, how you interpret their behaviors, what you feel about them and their actions and, most important, how you respond. If you learn nothing else about emotions from this book, learn this: you choose how you act. If, for example, you feel unmotivated working for a boss who doesn't appreciate you, realize that you are choosing to remain unmotivated. If you get irritated when your spouse leaves dirty dishes in the sink, remember that you are allowing yourself to be irritated. You can't always change other people, but you can usually change how you respond to them.

Recognizing emotional states (chapter 2)

There are two major components to recognizing emotions—recognizing emotions in yourself and recognizing them in others. This section discusses ways of improving in each area.

Recognizing your own emotions
I mentioned in chapter 2 that the biggest problem that most of us face in recognizing our own emotional states is that we sometimes do not focus enough attention on those states. In the hustle and bustle of everyday life we often find our attention pulled outwards as we try to deal with the many external challenges that life provides. Sometimes this can lead us to overlook signals from our body about important emotional states. Thus, the most effective methods for improving the ability to recognize our own emotions will focus on increasing either the *quantity* or *quality* of the attention we pay to our emotional states.

Appraise yourself The first step in becoming more emotionally intelligent is to conduct an honest appraisal of yourself. Begin with a general approach to your emotions and past experiences by completing the following statements. Consider how you feel as well as how you act, and how often these emotions occur.

- I am happy when:
- I am sad when:

- I am fearful when:
- I get frustrated by:
- I am angered by:
- I am excited when:
- I hate it when:
- I am lonely when:

Next, consider some specific past emotional situations and experiences. Examine those that were good as well as those that were bad, those that you handled well and those that you wish you could do all over again. Analyse your internal feelings as well as your outward behavior.

- Which emotions are easier for me to express? Which are more difficult? Why?
- What do my body language or nonverbal cues say about my emotional state?
- Do my reactions and behavior usually reflect how I *really* feel?
- Did I overlook or ignore cues about appropriate ways to behave?
- How might outcomes and relationships have been different had I reacted differently?

Monitor your emotional states frequently Frequent monitoring of your emotions should begin to lead you toward recognizing a feeling as it happens and, subsequently, to thoughtful and deliberate responses. Attend not only to *how* you felt (quality) but also to how frequently your emotions *change* (quantity). You could do this by keeping an "emotional diary" in which you record how you felt at various points throughout your day, what triggered those feelings and how you responded. Or in lieu of a diary, you might set aside a specific time each day in which to reflect on emotions. In the monitoring process, pay particular attention to:

- What you are feeling and why you are feeling it.
- The connection between what you are feeling and what you say or do.
- How what you are feeling affects your relationships with others.

Enlist the help of others You will find that other people are willing, even eager, to assist you because by helping you they're helping themselves. If you can learn to manage emotions—yours as well as those of others—more constructively, their lives and interactions with you will be filled with greater understanding and less tension and anger. Ask others for honest and direct feedback:

- How do they view you as an emotional person?
- How do they view your reactions and interactions with others in emotional situations?
- How does your self-appraisal compare with those offered by others?

- What are others' suggestions for how you can become a more emotionally intelligent person?

In your feedback sessions with others, emphasize that you value their honesty, observations and advice. Take notes and stay open-minded. Enlist others' continued support and ask them to hold you to your commitment to change.

Another way in which to get help from others is to use as role models those friends or colleagues who handle their emotions successfully. Ask them for advice and constructive criticism. In addition to providing you with emotional support, they may be especially insightful in regard to mutual acquaintances—they may, for instance, be coworkers who don't get upset by the boss who irritates you.

Recognizing the emotions of others

Recognizing emotions in others is a little different from recognizing your own because in addition to simply paying attention (which is still important!), it is also necessary to correctly decipher the cues that others give off and reach an accurate estimate of their mood.

Appraise others' emotions Attend to the behavior and expressions of others to ascertain their emotional states. As you did in your self-appraisal, consider a variety of past emotional situations and experiences.

- Which emotions in others am I able to accurately identify? On which do I need to work?
- What distinguishes those situations in which I am accurate in identifying emotions and those in which I am not?
- Am I more likely to attend to facial expressions, voice or body language?
- Do I assume that others' words are accurate reflections of their feelings and look no further for explanations of their behavior?
- How do I react to others in emotional situations?

Learn about emotions The table on the next page outlines six key emotions and the facial and body cues that distinguish them. These will help you to identify the emotional states of others so that you can respond most effectively. Additional resources on recognizing emotions are provided in the resources section (see page 175). You can also learn about emotions by studying the emotions of characters in books, TV shows and films. Test yourself by identifying emotions and predicting reactions as you observe the interactions of others in public places such as restaurants or at work. Remember that cues to a person's emotional state will be signalled by:

- Facial expressions (the eyes, mouth and forehead are particularly expressive).
- Eye contact or the lack of it.

Table 6.1: Recognizing Emotions

Emotion	Mouth	Eyes & Eyebrows	Voice & Speech	Head & Body
HAPPINESS	Smile; corners turned up, possibly exposing teeth	Crinkled skin at outside corners of eyes (crow's-feet)	Talk fast, loudly; laugh	Possibly dancing or jumping about; clapping; leaning back; arms open
SADNESS	Pouting or frowning; lips and jaw lowered	Crying; drooping eyelids; raised inner ends of eyebrows	Talk slightly slower; lower intensity; possible slurring; audible sighs	Slumped shoulders; flaccid muscles; hanging head; remaining motionless or passive
ANGER	Frown; tense jaw and mouth	Staring; contracted brows	Talk slightly faster and very much higher; abrupt and tense articulation; interrupt others	Head jerks; possible aggressive gestures (e.g., hands on hips, fist); flared nostrils; red or flushed face; body held erect
FEAR	Tense mouth; trembling lips; chattering teeth	Eyes wide open; fast blinking; crying	Talk much faster and very much higher; tense or irregular voice or breathing; possible screaming	Withdrawal or freeze reaction; squirming; sweaty palms; rigid muscles

Table 6.1: Recognizing Emotions (continued)

Emotion	Mouth	Eyes & Eyebrows	Voice & Speech	Head & Body
SURPRISE	Mouth open; corners turned slightly up	Eyes wide open; eyebrows raised and apart	Stunned silence or talk loudly, excitedly	May cover mouth with hands or freeze
DISGUST	Curled upper lip; tongue possibly visible	Lowered inner corners of the eyebrows	Talk much slower and lower; grumbled chest tone; guttural sounds (e.g., ugh)	Head moves backward or side to side; wrinkled nose

- Tone of voice.
- Body posture (e.g., shrinking away, arms crossed, leaning back).
- Difficulty staying in control.
- Physiological state (e.g., sweaty palms, tensed muscles, clenched jaw).
- Being especially argumentative or quiet.
- Appearing uninterested or distracted.

Monitor those around you frequently Just as you monitor your own emotional states in a diary or at specific times, examine those of others around you as well. Attend to not only how they feel, but also how frequently their emotions change and possible triggers. Examine:

- What others are feeling and why.
- The connection between what they are feeling and what they say or do.
- How what they are feeling affects your relationships with them.

Understanding emotions (chapter 3)

Once you're able to recognize emotions, the next step is to understand them. If in recognizing emotions you are attempting to ascertain "What" (as in "What is happening here?"), then understanding emotions can be viewed as your attempt to answer "Why" ("Why is everyone angry?"). The techniques already described as ways to improve emotional recognition can be helpful in improving emotional understanding as well.

Self-appraisal Additional insight into emotions can be garnered by continuing your self-appraisal of a variety of past emotional situations and experiences:

- Why am I feeling this way? What information or experiences have influenced how I feel?
- How do I typically react when faced with an emotional situation, and why?

- Given the variety of ways in which I might react in a particular emotional situation, why do I react as I do?
- What have been the personal and professional consequences of not understanding emotions (mine and those of others)?

Perspective taking Perspective taking is the process of putting yourself in another person's place and imagining what that person is thinking or feeling. Through perspective taking, you can come to understand the causes and effects of others' feelings. It lets you "experience" the emotional world of others.

Practice perspective taking by pretending that you are not you. Select a person quite different from you or one who has a different point of view. Mentally put yourself in the other's place and work to understand their point of view, motivation, thoughts and feelings. Answer the following questions as you think this person would:

- What information or experiences have influenced "my" perspective and emotions?
- How does "my" thinking and feeling affect "my" behavior?
- How do "I" typically react when faced with an emotional situation, and why?
- How do "I" want others to respond when "I" am in an emotional situation?

While perspective taking is important to understanding others, it is *critical* to anticipating how your own words and deeds will affect the feelings of others and their potential reactions. Anticipating how others might feel and behave, and being prepared for different reactions, is one of the core characteristics of the emotionally intelligent person. Before you enter (or instigate) a situation in which strong emotions are likely, use perspective taking and your new knowledge about emotions to consider:

- What emotions might arise and why?
- How are the people involved (including myself) likely to react and respond?
- How might I handle different emotional scenarios?

Regulating and controlling emotions (chapter 4)

We now turn to the matter of emotional regulation. Successfully managing emotions provides at least two significant benefits: first, it can be highly beneficial to mental and physical well-being, and second, it is a very important social skill. The ability to regulate emotions—both our own and those of others—is central to maintaining effective social relationships.

For the most part, we're concerned here with the need to manage potentially destructive emotions such as anger, disgust or sadness (for example, weeping uncontrollably during a stressful business meeting is generally something you want to avoid). It is less common that we need to inhibit or eliminate outward signs of positive emotions (although it is wise not to smile too broadly when holding an unbeatable poker hand). Most of the techniques that follow are thus aimed at managing destructive emotions.

Regulating your own emotions

Delay responding One of the simplest methods of emotional control is to *slow down* your responding. This does not mean avoiding the problem or ignoring other people. Rather it means giving yourself time to choose the right response by delaying your initial impulse. Delaying your first impulse will provide you (and others) with the time necessary to refocus on the issue at hand and express emotions in suitable and appropriate ways.

There are a variety of ways to delay responding in an emotional situation. Some are aimed at getting control of yourself, while others allow everyone some time and space to calm down and reflect. Changing the subject is a simple and often effective way to delay responding. Inhaling and exhaling deeply and slowly will delay responding while at the same time calming your physiological reactions. Just plain silence will allow you to steady yourself while observing the other person in order to understand their perspective.

Taking a "time out" is another way to delay responding. If you are able to leave the situation for a short while, do something physical such as taking a walk around the building or jogging in a secluded hallway. Listening to music or perusing a book of inspirational quotations—or any other favorite book—are also good options. For those times when you are unable to physically leave a situation (for example, an important business meeting), slowly count to ten or twenty—or higher if necessary. Establish in advance (perhaps during your self-appraisal described earlier) what you will do in a time out, and practice it so that it will feel natural and automatic when the time comes to use it.

Whether you delay responding by changing the subject, requesting a time out or just saying nothing, your goal is the same: to replace out-of-control or harmful emotions with thoughtful responses and constructive action. Make good use of the time you have gained:

- Remind yourself: "I control my emotions; they don't control me."
- Work to develop a thorough understanding of the situation by gathering additional information, talking to others or taking the perspective of others.
- Actively plan your next steps.

Use cognitive reappraisal Your interpretation of the situation determines your emotional reaction. Cognitive reappraisal means redefining a situation to produce a more desirable emotional state. For most of us, coming up with alternative ways of interpreting our world is not something we undertake routinely. But by becoming aware of how your perceptions can influence feelings and behavior, you can respond more effectively. Consider, for example, a recent instance in which you were angry.

- Could the situation have been perceived in a different way?
- Are there alternative explanations for why the individuals involved behaved as they did?
- Would you have become angry if you'd interpreted the situation differently?
- Most important, were your original perceptions accurate?

Cognitive reappraisal is a key component of emotional lesson 2 (see page 136). By redefining the situation, you are exerting control over how you perceive others, how you interpret their behaviors, what you feel about them and their actions and, subsequently, how you respond. Through cognitive reappraisal, you may discover new ways of interpreting emotions and understanding people.

Shift attention Another emotional regulation technique involves changing the focus of your attention so that instead of concentrating on the distressing problem, you focus your attention on something less arousing. For example, you might take a brief "mental trip" by envisaging a peaceful, calm setting such as a beach or mountain stream, and then imagining that you are really there and away from all tension and emotional distress. Of course, shifting attention does not have to be as elaborate as this—simply thinking about *anything* else (your pet; last night's dinner) can be an improvement over fixating on a distressing event.

Express anger appropriately One of the most troublesome emotions, and one that frequently needs controlling, is anger. As we have seen, however, anger, like other emotions, *is* controllable. For instance, while you might often be angry at your boss, you seldom if ever yell at him because you fear the consequences enough either to swallow your anger or to express it in a suitable manner. If you can control your anger in some situations, *and you can*, then you can control it in others. Feeling angry is fine, but expressing anger in a hostile and aggressive manner is not. Your goal is to control the anger you feel and express it in a more acceptable manner.

Controlling your anger in the heat of the moment takes place on two fronts—the internal and the external. Both battles necessitate buying yourself some time to calm down and refocus. (Research on the physiology of stress indicates that most people require twenty minutes to calm down—that's how long it takes for your heart rate to return to normal.) If you feel yourself about to erupt, STOP! Practice saying: "I need a time out before proceeding."

Once you've gained some time, use it. On the internal front:

- Remind yourself that "angry" is not the image you want to present.
- Repeat to yourself this mantra: "I am in control and the anger I feel will pass."
- Reframe "You make me angry" to "I will deal with my anger constructively."

Slow your anger with controlled deep breathing. When calmer, ask yourself:

- Is this situation similar to an experience from my past?
- How important is my relationship with this person?
- What other things are going on in my life right now that might be contributing to how I am currently feeling?
- What's at risk in this situation?
- Is my anger hiding some underlying problem that is really at the root of what's going on?

Externally, you want to present the image that you are composed and in control of yourself, your thoughts and your actions. When you are ready:

151

- Explain that you are angry and why, and that you want to discuss and resolve the issue. Practice saying things like: "I am angry because ..." or "Although I am angry, I want to discuss this calmly."
- Begin sentences with "I" rather than "You."
- Express your anger as "disappointment" at the person's actions and the consequences of those actions, rather than directing anger at the person's personality or intellect.
- Balance any expressed anger with care, concern and appreciation. Ensure that the relationship is back on track.
- Don't yell. Increasing your volume will only escalate emotions and conflict.

Pent-up anger and other unexpressed emotions can be quite stressful but can be reduced through relaxation techniques such as massage, meditation or yoga, vigorous physical exercise, or involvement in outside hobbies or interests. Venting to trusted others is another way of coping. If you have tried all (or at least most) of these techniques and are still unable to express your emotions appropriately, you might consider other options: an anger-management class, self-assertiveness training or seeking help from a competent professional. This is particularly recommended if your emotions and how you handle them continue to be detrimental to your personal and professional relationships, are harmful to your health and well-being, or are holding you back from being the person you want to be.

Regulating emotions in others

A big part of being an emotionally intelligent person is understanding and regulating emotions in yourself, but the *real* work comes in understanding and regulating the emotions of others. Being emotionally intelligent means comforting, encouraging, motivating and calming others as you build relationships, reduce tension and resolve conflicts.

Coping with emotional distress (yours as well as others') can, admittedly, be difficult and stress inducing. You may be faced with anger, sadness, disdain, tears and yelling—all in the space of a few seconds. The emotions may be directed at bosses, family, friends, the situation, the world, or, most painful of all, you. It could all be as overwhelming for you as it is for the person you're trying to help. If, however, you can remain calm and attentive, you will be able to discern what the other person needs: sympathy, comfort, commiseration or just someone to listen. Because everyone differs in their level of sensitivity and comfort with physical contact, it is not advisable to pat, hug or otherwise touch a distressed coworker or someone you do not know well. Listening will often be the first, best and sometimes only thing you can do.

Active listening Active listening means being attentive and working to understand the message and emotions being expressed. It means attending to verbal as well as nonverbal cues. In terms of emotional regulation, the most important things about active listening are: 1) it makes the speaker feel free to talk openly and honestly, and 2) it makes the speaker feel that he or she is being understood. To make certain you understand what the other person is saying and feeling:

- Ask open-ended questions rather than questions that can be answered yes or no.
- Don't be afraid of silence—after asking a question, wait long enough to let the other person answer at their own pace.
- Ask for examples to clarify.
- Restate or summarize what you think has been said.
- Let the other person know when you understand and when you don't.

Reach out In addition to careful listening, reaching out to the other person can often repair emotional damage. This may be especially important when your own words or actions have contributed to the other's distress. Reaching out can take several forms: calming the other person down, soothing hurt feelings or making amends. While you may sometimes feel that repairing emotions is time-consuming or unnecessary (or in the workplace, inappropriately personal), consider the consequences of not doing so: protracted distress and conflict, mistrust and ruined relationships.

Reaching out early and often can prevent serious problems from developing.

In reaching out, use the techniques of perspective taking, active listening and delaying responding described earlier. In addition, open the lines of communication:

- Directly acknowledge the emotions of others and their emotional needs.
- Encourage them to openly and honestly express their emotions. Don't interrupt.
- Be sure you understand the other's position and feelings. Ask questions.
- *Never* say someone is wrong to feel the way they are feeling. Be accepting and respectful.
- If you are the cause of the other's emotional distress, admit your responsibility and apologize sincerely. Ask what you can do to make amends.

Use humor Humor can enhance general well-being, prolong a good mood or lighten a sad moment. It can defuse a tense or angry situation, distract attention to something less distressing or serve as a means of delaying a potentially destructive response. Humor can, however, also backfire or be misinterpreted, making a difficult emotional situation worse. In trying to address an emotional situation with humor, do so without poking fun at others. Make sure that the joke's on you; have a sense of humor about yourself. And remember, the first rule of comedy is "timing is everything"—choose your moment.

Using emotions effectively (chapter 5)

Finally, we come to the issue of using emotions effectively in your life. This turns out to be the most difficult component of emotional intelligence about which to give practical advice. One reason for this is that all of the techniques for recognizing, understanding and regulating emotions discussed up to this point in this chapter are also relevant to using emotions effectively: appraisal of yourself and others, frequent monitoring of emotional states, perspective taking, active listening, open communication, delay responding, cognitive reappraisal, shifting attention and reaching out. Many of the techniques for using emotions effectively have therefore already been discussed. Another reason is that chapter 5 has already described a number of specific examples of how to use emotions in order to enhance goal performance, improve general well-being and influence others.

There are, however, some additional tips about using emotions to handle conflict better. The ability to manage and successfully resolve conflict is not only a key leadership skill but also an important part of maintaining healthy relationships outside the workplace.

Express hidden emotions It's important to keep in mind that providing information about how you feel and why can be useful to others. As mentioned in chapter 5, explaining your emotional state tells others that they and the issue under discussion are important to you. The trick is to express your emotions in a way that is appropriate and informative. Begin with some self-appraisal:

- Are there certain kinds of emotion that are more difficult for me to express than others?
- Have there been times when hiding my emotions interfered in resolving a conflict or having a healthy relationship?
- Do I tend to blame others for feeling as I do?

During a conflict, be sure you know the thoughts and feelings that you want to communicate to the other party. This sounds simple, but conflicts often produce an avalanche of emotions, and you should think clearly about what you want to express.

- Determine why you are feeling as you do. What specific features of the conflict are making you feel angry, frustrated or ignored? Is it the behavior of the other person, what's been said, the temperature in the room or something completely outside the current situation?
- Will expressing your emotions be beneficial to the conflict resolution process?
- Are you providing the other person with useful information about how you feel and why?

- Once your emotions have been expressed, is there something that the other person can do about how you feel?

When you are ready to explain how you feel and why:

- Choose your words carefully. Be courteous and calm, not out of control.
- Be specific: "I feel bad" is not very informative. Instead say: "I am frustrated (or angry or disappointed, etc.) because . . ." The more explanation you can provide, the more informative it will be.
- Don't blame the other person for how *you* feel. For instance, say, "I am hurt by this situation" rather than "You hurt my feelings."
- Explain diplomatically and respectfully what the other person can do to improve the situation or relationship.
- If you feel you're about to cry, get angry or otherwise inappropriately express your emotions, remind yourself of the image you want to project and that your goal is to build a rewarding and positive relationship.

Confront conflict constructively Resolving conflicts can be a challenging process. It requires effort, patience, open communication, negotiation, management of emotions and creative solutions. Successful conflict resolution is a collaborative process that is constructive and fair and produces satisfactory solutions for everyone.

- Express your sincere desire to resolve the conflict. Agree to communicate frankly and openly.
- Address the problem directly but not aggressively. If there is more than one problem, tackle the problems one at a time, starting with the easiest one to resolve.
- Identify points of mutual agreement and emphasize the need to work *together* for a mutually satisfactory solution.
- Cooperate and compromise. Keep in mind that your goal is not to win, but rather to have a healthy, productive and continuing relationship that will benefit everyone involved.
- Throughout the conflict resolution process, monitor and directly address all parties' emotional states, particularly anger and distress.
- Focus on the future. Emphasize intentions, goals and opportunities rather than past behaviors and problems.

To sum up

Once you have settled upon a method, or a set of methods, to improve some portion of your EQ, the hard work begins. It is relatively easy to decide to change, and even to come up with a plan for change, but the hard work lies in actually making that change happen. Here are three final pieces of advice before you begin any such efforts.

Establish goals

Based on what you learned about yourself and emotions in general, establish your goals and list them.

- What changes have the greatest priority (e.g., expressing hidden emotions, controlling anger, attending to the emotional states of others)?
- What actions will most address the concerns of others?
- What changes, if not made, will be detrimental to your personal and professional relationships?

Place the list of goals in a place where you will see them frequently. Keep a logbook or journal to track your progress. Frequently evaluate how you are doing and what lessons you have learned, and, most important, if you have not been making progress, determine why not.

Commit to change

Commit to becoming an emotionally intelligent person. Envisage how you want to be and mentally rehearse the "New You" until you feel comfortable with it. Publicly commit to making changes by telling others you are trying to change; ask for their help and support as you strive to become a more emotionally intelligent person.

It is always more difficult to back down from a commitment once it has been made public, so letting the most important people in your life know that you are making this effort will tend to keep you committed to the goal.

Keep reassessing yourself
Becoming an emotionally intelligent person will take time and will require an ongoing reassessment of how you are doing and where you can improve. Evaluate yourself and seek feedback from trusted others:

- What did I do well?
- What areas still need improvement?
- Was I attentive to verbal and nonverbal cues?
- Did I work to understand the other person's emotions and position?
- Was I accurate in my perspective taking?
- Was I honest and informative when expressing my feelings?
- Was I in control of my emotions or were they in control of me?

SCORING AND INTERPRETING YOUR EQ TESTS

Self-report tests

Once you have completed the self-report tests, you can score them using the instructions (provided below) for each particular test. For each self-report test there are five items that indicate **high** EQ, and five that indicate **low** EQ. The instructions for each test tell you how to combine these items to produce your score for that test. The instructions also tell you how to interpret your total test score. *Be sure to read these instructions carefully, since the scoring interpretation changes from test to test.*

Multirater tests

You do not complete these tests yourself. Instead, you need to have at least one person who knows you well complete the test, answering the questions about *you*. It is even better to have several people complete the test, so that you can get a broader picture of how others view your EQ abilities. Once they have done so, you can score the tests using the instructions provided for each one. The system for scoring and interpreting these tests is similar to the one used for the self-report tests.

Performance tests

These tests are somewhat different from the others. You complete each of these yourself, selecting all the answers that you think are correct for each point. The scoring instructions for each of these tests tell you what the correct answers are, and how to calculate your score for each one. The instructions also tell you how to interpret your scores.

Interpreting your scores

You will have several different scores for most of the EQ components: a self-report score, one (or more) ratings by others and a performance score. How should you use all this information? The most important things to look for are consistent patterns in your scores. For example, if your self-report scores indicate that you are excellent in a particular area, your multirater scores indicate that you are good and your performance test is also in the good range, then you are safe in assuming that this EQ component is one of your strengths. Similarly, if your self-scores indicate that you are average in some area, but your multirater and performance tests are in the range of "room for improvement," then the overall pattern suggests that this EQ component is one that you should probably work on.

What about situations in which the different scores do not agree? There is no easy answer to this question—if the tests do not agree and the pattern is not clear and consistent, you cannot have as much confidence in any conclusion. However, one rule of thumb you should keep in mind is this: *other people are often better judges of our EQ than we are.* Thus, if the multirater scores are at odds with your self-report scores, you should seriously consider giving extra weight to the multirater tests. The reason for this is that other people are often in a better position than you are to really see how effective you are in dealing with emotions. We may sometimes think that we are controlling our anger, for example, but it may be clear to others that we are furious.

After you have determined your scores and looked for consistent patterns, you should have an idea of the areas in which you might need to improve. You should then do two things. First, carefully read the sections of chapter 6 that describe ways in which you can improve your weakest EQ skills. Second, consult Resources (see page 175), which lists books, Web sites and other useful links. This section is organized by topic, so that you can quickly identify the resources that are most appropriate for you. One final thing to keep in mind is this: even in areas where you are strong, it never hurts to keep trying to improve. You may therefore find it useful to look through the resources section even for those areas in which your scores are consistently high.

SELF-REPORT TESTS

Test 1: Recognizing your own emotions

Add together your numerical responses for questions 1, 3, 4, 5 and 8. Then from that sum, *subtract* your numerical responses for questions 2, 6, 7, 9 and 10. The resulting value will be a score somewhere between −20 and +20.

$$
\begin{aligned}
\text{Excellent} &= \text{15 and above} \\
\text{Good} &= \text{10 to 14} \\
\text{Average} &= \text{1 to 9} \\
\text{Room for improvement} &= \text{Zero and below}
\end{aligned}
$$

Test 2: Recognizing emotions in others

Add together your numerical responses for questions 1, 2, 5, 6 and 9. Then from that sum, *subtract* your numerical responses for questions 3, 4, 7, 8 and 10. The resulting value will be a score somewhere between –20 and +20.

Excellent = 15 and above
Good = 10 to 14
Average = 1 to 9
Room for improvement = Zero and below

Test 4: Understanding the causes of your own emotions

Add together your numerical responses for questions 1, 2, 3, 6 and 9. Then from that sum, *subtract* your numerical responses for questions 4, 5, 7, 8 and 10. The resulting value will be a score somewhere between –20 and +20.

Excellent = 15 and above
Good = 10 to 14
Average = 1 to 9
Room for improvement = Zero and below

Test 6: Understanding the causes of others' emotions

Add together your numerical responses for questions 1, 3, 6, 7 and 9. Then from that sum, *subtract* your numerical responses for questions 2, 4, 5, 8 and 10. The resulting value will be a score somewhere between –20 and +20.

Excellent = 15 and above
Good = 10 to 14
Average = 1 to 9
Room for improvement = Zero and below

Test 8: Understanding the consequences of your own emotions

Add together your numerical responses for questions 1, 2, 3, 5 and 8. Then from that sum, *subtract* your numerical responses for questions 4, 6, 7, 9 and 10. The resulting value will be a score somewhere between −20 and +20.

Excellent = 15 and above
Good = 10 to 14
Average = 1 to 9
Room for improvement = Zero and below

Test 10: Understanding the consequences of others' emotions

Add together your numerical responses for questions 1, 2, 4, 6 and 9. Then from that sum, *subtract* your numerical responses for questions 3, 5, 7, 8 and 10. The resulting value will be a score somewhere between −20 and +20.

Excellent = 15 and above
Good = 10 to 14
Average = 1 to 9
Room for improvement = Zero and below

Test 13: Regulating your own emotions

Add together your numerical responses for questions 1, 5, 7, 9 and 10. Then from that sum, *subtract* your numerical responses for questions 2, 3, 4, 6 and 8. The resulting value will be a score somewhere between –20 and +20.

$$
\begin{aligned}
\text{Excellent} &= \text{11 and above} \\
\text{Good} &= \text{3 to 10} \\
\text{Average} &= \text{–4 to 2} \\
\text{Room for improvement} &= \text{–5 and below}
\end{aligned}
$$

Test 16: Regulating others' emotions

Add together your numerical responses for questions 1, 2, 4, 6 and 10. Then from that sum, *subtract* your numerical responses for questions 3, 5, 7, 8 and 9. The resulting value will be a score somewhere between –20 and +20.

$$
\begin{aligned}
\text{Excellent} &= \text{15 and above} \\
\text{Good} &= \text{10 to 14} \\
\text{Average} &= \text{1 to 9} \\
\text{Room for improvement} &= \text{Zero and below}
\end{aligned}
$$

Test 19: Using your own emotions

Add together your numerical responses for questions 1, 3, 5, 7 and 9. Then from that sum, *subtract* your numerical responses for questions 2, 4, 6, 8 and 10. The resulting value will be a score somewhere between –20 and +20.

$$\begin{aligned}
\text{Excellent} &= \text{11 and above} \\
\text{Good} &= \text{3 to 10} \\
\text{Average} &= \text{-4 to 2} \\
\text{Room for improvement} &= \text{-5 and below}
\end{aligned}$$

Test 21: Using others' emotions

Add together your numerical responses for questions 1, 4, 5, 6 and 7. Then from that sum, *subtract* your numerical responses for questions 2, 3, 8, 9 and 10. The resulting value will be a score somewhere between −20 and +20.

$$\begin{aligned}
\text{Excellent} &= \text{11 and above} \\
\text{Good} &= \text{3 to 10} \\
\text{Average} &= \text{-4 to 2} \\
\text{Room for improvement} &= \text{-5 and below}
\end{aligned}$$

MULTIRATER TESTS

Test 3: Recognizing emotions in others

Add together the rater's numerical responses for questions 1, 2, 4, 6 and 9. Then from that sum, *subtract* the rater's numerical responses for questions 3, 5, 7, 8 and 10. The resulting value will be a score somewhere between −20 and +20.

$$\begin{aligned} \text{Excellent} &= \text{16 and above} \\ \text{Good} &= \text{11 to 15} \\ \text{Average} &= \text{1 to 10} \\ \text{Room for improvement} &= \text{Zero and below} \end{aligned}$$

Test 7: Understanding the causes of others' emotions

Add together the rater's numerical responses for questions 1, 2, 6, 8 and 10. Then from that sum, *subtract* the rater's numerical responses for questions 3, 4, 5, 7 and 9. The resulting value will be a score somewhere between –20 and +20.

$$\begin{aligned} \text{Excellent} &= \text{5 and above} \\ \text{Good} &= \text{1 to 4} \\ \text{Average} &= \text{–4 to 0} \\ \text{Room for improvement} &= \text{–5 and below} \end{aligned}$$

Test 11: Understanding the consequences of others' emotions

Add together the rater's numerical responses for questions 1, 2, 6, 8 and 10. Then from that sum, *subtract* the rater's numerical responses for questions 3, 4, 5, 7 and 9. The resulting value will be a score somewhere between –20 and +20.

$$\begin{aligned} \text{Excellent} &= \text{16 and above} \\ \text{Good} &= \text{9 to 15} \end{aligned}$$

Average = −4 to 8
Room for improvement = −5 and below

Test 14: Regulating your own emotions

Add together the rater's numerical responses for questions 1, 2, 4, 5 and 6. Then from that sum, *subtract* the rater's numerical responses for questions 3, 7, 8, 9 and 10. The resulting value will be a score somewhere between −20 and +20.

Excellent = 10 and above
Good = 1 to 9
Average = −9 to 0
Room for improvement = −10 and below

Test 17: Regulating others' emotions

Add together the rater's numerical responses for questions 1, 3, 4, 7 and 9. Then from that sum, *subtract* the rater's numerical responses for questions 2, 5, 6, 8 and 10. The resulting value will be a score somewhere between −20 and +20.

Excellent = 16 and above
Good = 9 to 15
Average = −4 to 8
Room for improvement = −5 and below

Test 22: Using others' emotions

Add together the rater's numerical responses for questions 1, 2, 5, 6 and 7. Then from that sum, *subtract* the rater's numerical responses for questions 3, 4, 8, 9 and 10. The resulting value will be a score somewhere between –20 and +20.

Excellent = 10 and above
Good = 5 to 9
Average = –4 to 4
Room for improvement = –5 and below

PERFORMANCE TESTS

For each of the performance tests listed below, you will find the correct answers to the questions making up that test. Give yourself 5 points for each correct answer that you circled. For each answer that you circled that is *not* listed, subtract 5 points. Your resulting score should be interpreted in the following manner:

Excellent = 90 and above
Good = 75 to 85
Average = 45 to 70
Room for improvement = 40 and below

Test 5: Understanding the causes of your own emotions

1.	a,b,c	5.	a,b	8.	d
2.	a,d	6.	a,b	9.	a,d
3.	c,d	7.	c,d	10.	a,b
4.	b,c				

Test 9: Understanding the consequences of your own emotions

1.	a,b,d	5.	a,d	8.	a,b
2.	c,d	6.	d	9.	a,b
3.	b,c	7.	a,d	10.	a,d
4.	a,d				

Test 12: Understanding the consequences of others' emotions

1.	b,c	5.	a,d	8.	b,c,d
2.	a,c,d	6.	b,c	9.	a,b
3.	a,d	7.	a	10.	a,b
4.	c				

Test 15: Regulating your own emotions

1.	a,c,d	5.	c	8.	a,d
2.	b,c	6.	b,d	9.	c,d
3.	b,d	7.	a,d	10.	b,c
4.	b,c				

Test 18: Regulating others' emotions

1.	a,c,d	5.	a,b	8.	b,d
2.	a,c	6.	a,b	9.	a,c
3.	a,c	7.	c	10.	a,b
4.	c,d				

Test 20: Using your own emotions

1.	b,c,d	5.	a,b,d	8.	a,b
2.	c,d	6.	a,c	9.	c,d
3.	c	7.	a,b,d	10.	c
4.	b				

Test 23: Using others' emotions

1.	b,d	5.	d	8.	a,b
2.	a,b	6.	a,b	9.	b,c
3.	c,d	7.	b,c,d	10.	b
4.	a,b,c				

RESOURCES

GENERAL

Web sites

http://eqi.org/
Emotional Intelligence (EQ) offers practical advice for increasing social skills, self-control and motivation at work and home.

http://eiconsortium.org/
Emotional Intelligence Consortium describes components of emotional competence and summarizes research findings and articles.

www.selfgrowth.com/
SelfGrowth.com provides information and advice on being

successful in many realms of life as well as information and
links on EQ, IQ and related topics.

Books

*Emotional Intelligence at Work: The Untapped Edge of
Success* by H. Weisinger, Jossey Bass Wiley, 2000. How to
improve the components of emotional intelligence, including
self-motivation, mood management and emotional
mentoring.

*The Emotional Intelligence Activity Book: 50 Activities for
Promoting EQ at Work* by A. B. Lynn, Amacom, 2001.
Provides trainers and coaches with EQ exercises for use with
individuals or groups.

Executive EQ by R. Cooper and A. Sawaf, Texere
Publishing, 1997. Examination of emotions in business, and
how to recognize and control emotions in yourself as well as
in others.

On the Job: Emotional IQ, Student Workshop, book and
videotape set, Sunburst Communications, 2000. Exercises
and tip sheets for being emotionally intelligent at work.

Working with Emotional Intelligence by D. Goleman,
Bloomsbury, 1999. Workplace and skills for managing
feelings, interactions and communication, including
motivation, self-control, teamwork and leadership.

Recognizing Emotions

Web sites

http://psychology.about.com/library/
Tips and information on many aspects of psychology and relationships including suggestions for using nonverbal communication to improve relationships.

http://npin.org/library/2003/n00798/n00798.html
The article "Five Steps of Emotion Coaching" available at the Web site of the *National Parent Information Network* describes techniques for building a child's emotional intelligence.

Books

Emotions Revealed: Recognizing Faces and Feelings to Improve Communication and Emotional Life by P. Ekman, Times Books, 2003. A guide to recognizing emotions.

Hot Buttons: How to Resolve Conflict and Cool Everyone Down by S. Evans and S. S. Cohen, HarperCollins, 2001. Avoiding conflict by recognizing what pushes your buttons and by learning how not to push others' buttons.

I Know What You're Thinking: Using the Four Codes of Reading People to Improve Your Life by L. Glass, John Wiley & Sons, 2002. A guide to understanding the codes of communication—verbal, facial, body language and speech.

CD-ROM

The Micro Expression Training Tool by P. Ekman trains the user to recognize seven universal emotional expressions (available at www.emotionsrevealed.com).

Understanding Emotions

Web sites

http://psychology.about.com/library
Find tips and information on many aspects of psychology and relationships including being an excellent listener.

www.selfgrowth.com/
SelfGrowth.com provides information and advice on being successful in many realms of life including EQ, communication skills and goal setting.

Books

Coping with Difficult Bosses by R. Bramson, Nicholas Brealey Publishing Ltd, 1993, and *Coping With Difficult People* by R. Bramson, Career Press, 1981. Why bosses and others bully, stall, manipulate, complain, etc., and how to change your interactions with them.

Difficult Conversations: How to Discuss What Matters Most by D. Stone, B. Patton, S. Heen and R. Fisher, Penguin, 2000. Communication skills for confrontations.

Fierce Conversations: Achieving Success in Work and in Life, One Conversation at a Time by S. Scott, Piatkus Books, 2002. Anecdotes and exercises aimed at teaching communication and listening skills.

Opening Up: The Healing Power of Expressing Emotions by J. W. Pennebaker, Guilford Publications, 1997. Presents evidence for health benefits of expressing emotions as well as advice on opening up.

Toxic People:10 Ways of Dealing with People Who Make Your Life Miserable by L. Glass, St. Martin's Press, 1995. Difficult people, why they act as they do, and how to handle them.

Regulating Emotions

Web sites

www.angermgmt.com/
angermgmt.com provides a toolkit for measuring your anger along with advice and resources for coping with anger.

http://www.anger-management.net/index.cfm
Controlling the Volcano Within answers questions on anger and its management.

www.muextension.missouri.edu/xplor/hesguide/humanrel/
University of Missouri provides many articles related to human relations, including stress management and emotional well-being.

www.prosperityplace.com
Prosperity Place provides meditation instructions as well as advice on managing emotions and ways to soothe and improve your mind and body.

Books

Anger and Conflict in the Workplace: Spot the Signs, Avoid the Trauma by L. McClure, Impact Publications, 2000. How to handle anger and conflicts—your own and others.

The Anger Trap: Free Yourself from the Frustrations That Sabotage Your Life by L. Carter, Josey Bass Wiley, 2003. Understanding the causes of anger and how to break the destructive cycles of criticism, frustration and irritation.

Honor Your Anger: How Transforming Your Anger Style Can Change Your Life by B. Engel, John Wiley & Sons, 2002. A step-by-step process of discovering your "anger style," identifying its impact on your life, and learning to use your anger as a force for positive change.

Using Emotions

Web sites

www.confidencecenter.com
The Confidence Center provides articles on numerous topics related to the workplace including communication, negotiation, dealing with difficult people and goal setting.

www.mapfornonprofits.org
Handling Difficult People links you to articles, libraries and
online discussion groups related to difficult people, conflict
management and interpersonal skills.

www.NextLevelSciences.com
Next Level Sciences provides information and advice on the
science and psychology of setting and achieving goals in all
walks of life.

www.conflictdynamics.org
Conflict Dynamics provides information and other resources
related to conflict, building healthy relationships and
managing emotions.

www.shpm.com/articles/
Self-Help & Psychology Magazine contains articles and
advice for coping with conflict, stress, relationships and
health.

Books

The *Coward's Guide to Conflict: Empowering Solutions for
Those Who Would Rather Run Than Fight* by T. E. Ursiny,
Sourcebooks. Case studies, checklists and exercises for
teaching new ways to handle conflict.

*Creating Harmonious Relationships: A Practical Guide to the
Power of True Empathy* by A. LeCompte, Atlantic Books,
2000. Building relationships and turning conflict into
understanding.

Resources

The Emotional Revolution: Harnessing the Power of Your Emotions for a More Positive Life, by N. E. Rosenthal, Citadel Press, 2003. Guidelines on using emotions for a healthier, happier life.

How to Win Friends and Influence People by D. Carnegie, Pocket Books, revised edition 1981. First published in 1936, this classic is still relevant today.

The Power of Positive Confrontation by B. Pachter with S. Magee, Marlowe & Co, 2001. Positive approaches to confrontational situations.

Psychological Foundations of Success by S. J. Kraus, ChangePlanet Press, 2002. Based on decades of research on success and well-being, this book presents a five-step system for personal achievement.

REFERENCES

Bramson, R. (1993). *Coping with Difficult Bosses.* London: Nicholas Brealey Publishing Ltd.

Capobianco, S., Davis, M.H. and Kraus, L.A. (2003). *Managing Conflict Dynamics: A Practical Approach.* St. Petersburg, FL: Eckerd College Management Development Institute.

Carver, C. S., Scheier, M. F. and Weintraub, J. K. (1989). "Assessing coping strategies: a theoretically based approach." *Journal of Personality and Social Psychology*, 56, 267–83.

Chernis, C. (2000). "Emotional intelligence: what it is and why it matters." Paper presented at the annual meeting of the Society for Industrial and Organizational Psychology, New Orleans, LA.

Davies, M., Stankov, L. and Roberts, R.D. (1998). "Emotional intelligence: in search of an elusive construct." *Journal of*

Personality and Social Psychology, 75, 989–1015.

Franzoi, S.L. (2000). *Social Psychology* (2nd edition). Boston, McGraw-Hill.

Glass, L. (1995). *Toxic People:10 Ways of Dealing with People Who Make Your Life Miserable*. New York: St. Martin's Press.

Gohm, C. L. and Clore, G. L. (2002). "Affect as information: an individual-differences approach." In L.F. Barrett and P. Salovey (eds.), *The Wisdom in Feeling: Psychological Processes in Emotional Intelligence* (pp. 89–113). New York: The Guilford Press.

Goleman, D. (1996). *Emotional Intelligence: Why It Can Matter More Than IQ*. London: Bloomsbury Publishing.

Goleman, D. (1999). *Working with Emotional Intelligence*. London: Bloomsbury Publishing.

Gross, J. J. and John, O. P. (2002). "Wise emotional regulation." In L. F. Barrett and P. Salovey (eds.), *The Wisdom in Feeling: Psychological Processes in Emotional Intelligence* (pp. 297–318). New York: The Guilford Press.

Jones, E.E. (1990). *Interpersonal Perception*. New York: W. H. Freeman.

Mayer, J. D., Salovey, P., Caruso, D. R. and Sitarenios, G. (2003). "Measuring emotional intelligence with the MSCEIT V2.0." *Emotion*, 3, 97–105.

Picard, R. (1997). *Affective Computing*. Cambridge, MA: The MIT Press.

Roberts, R. D., Zeidner, M. and Mathews, G. (2001). "Does emotional intelligence meet traditional standards for an intelligence? Some new data and conclusions." *Emotion*, 1, 196–231.

"Sadness," "Happiness," "Fear," "Anger," "Disgust" Web sites

accessed 17 September, 2003, at: members.aol.com/
nonverbal2. D. B. Givens, Center for Nonverbal Studies,
copyright 1998–2001.

Salovey, P. and Mayer, J. D. (1990). "Emotional intelligence."
Imagination, Cognition, and Personality, 9, 185–211.

Schilling, D. (1996). *50 Activities for Teaching Emotional
Intelligence, Level II: Middle School*. Jalmar Books.

Schwarz, N. and Clore, G. L. (1983). "Mood, misattribution,
and judgments of well-being: informative and directive
functions of affective states." *Journal of Personality and
Social Psychology*, 45, 513–23.

Schwarz, N. and Clore, G. L. (1988). "How do I feel about
it? Informative functions of affective states." In K. Fiedler
and J. Forgas (eds.), *Affect, Cognition, and Social Behavior*
(pp. 44–62). Toronto: Hogrefe International.

Tugade, M. M. and Fredrickson, B. L. (2002). "Positive
emotions and emotional intelligence." In L.F. Barrett and
P. Salovey (eds.), *The Wisdom in Feeling: Psychological
Processes in Emotional Intelligence* (pp. 319–40). New
York: The Guilford Press.

Wilson, T.D. (2002). *Strangers to Ourselves: Discovering the
Adaptive Unconscious*. Cambridge, MA: The Belknap Press
of Harvard University Press.

INDEX

Index

Index